Ratty Restored

A Vole, a Mink and a Man

Mel Rockett

Published by New Generation Publishing in 2024

Copyright © Mel Rockett 2024

First Edition

The author asserts the moral right under the Copyright, Designs and Patents Act 1988 to be identified as the author of this work.

All Rights reserved. No part of this publication may be reproduced, stored in a retrieval system or transmitted, in any form or by any means without the prior consent of the author, nor be otherwise circulated in any form of binding or cover other than that which it is published and without a similar condition being imposed on the subsequent purchaser.

ISBN: 978-1-83563-532-2

www.newgeneration-publishing.com

New Generation Publishing

Foreword

This is the story of one man's experience with a large-scale water vole reintroduction project in Northumberland's Kielder Forest. I am not an expert in any branch of the natural sciences. I have no scientific background, and this story is not intended as an exhaustive report on how successful or not the project has been. It is the story of ten years of experience as a volunteer and the joy this has given me. I have gained a huge amount from this and other volunteer activities with Northumberland Wildlife Trust, and by sharing these activities with many colleagues and friends. So, this book is a celebration. In it I attempt to convey something of the facts about water voles, mink and volunteering, but mostly I want to illustrate the benefits for nature and for people of such an undertaking. I hope you enjoy it.

Nothing here represents the views of Northumberland Wildlife Trust, Forestry England, Tyne Rivers Trust or anyone else.

Contents

Foreword iii
Chapter 1 Neville's Demise! 1
Chapter 2 Neville the Water Vole 6
Chapter 3 Neville's Nemesis 16
Chapter 4 Friends of Neville 25
Chapter 5 Neville's New Home 34
Chapter 6 Guarding Neville's New Home 51
Chapter 7 Where Neville Came From. 74
Chapter 8 Neville Away! 86
Chapter 9 Company for Neville 98
Chapter 10 Where's Neville? 110
Chapter 11 They Came to See Neville. I'm A Celebrity Get Me to Kielder 122
Chapter 12 What Now for Neville? 127
APPENDIX 134

For Neville and all who follow him

"Weasels and stoats and foxes and so on. They're all right in a way… but they break out sometime, there's no denying it, and then, you can't really trust them, and that's a fact" ……add **American mink to the list.**
(Kenneth Grahame: *Wind in the Willows***)**

With special thanks to –

Graham Holyoak for his relentless support and advice in putting this book together

Kelly Hollings for her leadership and support

Sheila Cadge for her meticulous proof reading and..

especially to Cath for getting me out of the house so often.

Chapter 1

Neville's Demise!

I know I can be a bit over sentimental, but when I handled my very first water vole as he was checked out before being put in his release pen, I couldn't resist giving him a name. For some reason he looked like a Neville to me. He was one of the black-furred voles and quite large. This naming was a mistake.

On the first morning after the baffle board (I'll tell you later) had been fixed to his pen, we returned to feed the voles. As our van approached the release site, we noticed a large heron standing next to the pen. Startled, the heron took flight - and in his large, dagger-like beak we saw, yes, a large, black-furred water vole! Was it Neville? Very likely although he may have escaped - or been eaten earlier. We'll never know. But I knew.

View from a Volunteer
I think it was September 2014. It was early autumn anyway. A group of 16 potential volunteers gathered at EALS, the Forestry Commission's northern office in Bellingham, Northumberland. We were to be introduced to the project which came to be known as "Restoring Ratty". Not some attempt to convert non-believers to the delights of *Wind in the Willows*, but a serious scientific experiment in the re-introduction of the once-numerous water vole to the wilds of Kielder Forest.

The 16 included myself, Robin Bailey, Steve Harris, Don Learmouth, Jessica Sunderby, John Bower and others. Bigging up the project were Kelly Hollings and Kevin O'Hara of Northumberland

Wildlife Trust (NWT), and Tom Dearnley of the Forestry Commission. I had worked with Kelly for the last few years as a volunteer working on the Northumbrian Water sites at Bakethin and the surrounding area, and with Kevin on an otter survey. All good experiences which persuaded me to come along to this introductory session. Little did I know that I could be signing my life over to years of toil in control of a four-wheel drive as it careered round the Kielder Forest tracks which seemed to go on for miles. It has been a wonderful journey, with many rewarding experiences and lots of new acquaintances, some of whom I hope I can call new friends.

Was this Neville?

Let's be clear here. The water vole features in that iconic Victorian book *The Wind in the Willows*. Herein it is known as "Ratty" the water rat. But it is not a rat! It is a vole. And a vole is almost entirely a vegan. A rat certainly isn't. A vole is cute and cuddly. A rat is sharp and cunning. Got that? Vole good, rat - make your own mind up.

As a boy in North Lincolnshire, I was aware of the "water rat" as locals called it. Mainly because it was numerous around the many drainage dykes in the Isle of Axholme, close to my home(s) at various locations in and around Scunthorpe. It was so numerous and active that some blamed it for damaging the banks of the vital dykes which protected the surrounding low-lying land from flooding. Much of this land is at or below sea level, so the dykes are quite important to the locals. Close to the charmingly named village of Swinefleet, the damage was perceived to be so bad that local farmers would pay us sixpence for every dead vole we could produce. (A sixpence was worth 2.5p in modern money, aka "decimal currency". If you're still in your infancy, you may need to refer to history books here.) And I wasn't alone, for as the Rolling Stones sang in their song *Live with Me*: *My best friend he shoots water rats and feeds them to his geese*! Little did we know that a few decades later this beautiful little mammal would be so endangered, with 95% of the population gone. What happened?

Apart from a few schoolboys with air rifles, the main threats to the water vole came from modern farming and forestry practices and a new enemy - caused by the rise and decline of the fur industry. Wouldn't you just die for a mink fur coat? You would if you were an American mink bred on a fur farm in Ponteland. There were lots of other such farms around the UK. Some still exist in Europe. But by the 1990s the animal rights movement and general public sensitivity, with famous fashion models lending support, meant that fur sales were declining and these farms becoming unprofitable. What to do? Some farmers closed down and disposed of their mink population in humane and responsible ways. Others "found that their mink had escaped" or claimed that they had been released by animal rights activists. Perhaps some had been. Either way it was a disaster for local wildlife. Mink are highly successful predators. Beautiful and awe-inspiring in the way that many predators are.

This morning, I was privileged and appalled to watch a female sparrowhawk take and devour a collared dove in my garden. It took a second for her to make the kill and then she sat there looking around. I'm sure she could see or sense me watching from my window a dozen or so feet away. She decided to ignore me and began plucking away the dove's feathers. This took at least 20 minutes and during this time she ignored several vehicles passing by. Eventually she seemed satisfied and flew up with the prepared meal in her talons. I thought that was all I would see.

She was off somewhere safer to enjoy her meal. So, still wonderstruck I wandered off to make a cup of tea. When I returned to the window, I was surprised to see that she had only flown off a few feet and had then settled in the shelter of the hedge to enjoy her meal. I was transfixed as she began to tear the carcass apart and steadily work her way through the feast. It took her a further 30 minutes. With each bite she would look up and cast around with those striking eyes. All I could do was stay still and wonder. The power in her upper leg muscles and those talons were awesome. Finally, she'd had her fill and flew off, but not without the little that remained of the unfortunate dove. She obviously wasn't leaving the scraps for anyone else. A lesson in the cruel beauty of some aspects of our natural world. And a lesson I think in not getting too anthropomorphic about our relationship with animals. I could have been distressed at the fate of the dove. I love to see them in the garden. And I could have been horrified at the violence of the hawk. But this is just nature. The same ecosystem which we are also a part of.

Back to those mink. Whatever the reason for their escape the American mink were soon causing mayhem in the surrounding areas. Moving along the riparian routeways provided by our extensive dendritic system, the mink were soon ravaging the whole county. This was a new predator in the system and local wildlife was unprepared and lacked defence. Some species were very badly hit, our water voles being one of the worst affected. Did it matter? Yes. Water voles are a keystone species in the food chain, providing lots of protein for native predators such as stoat, heron, tawny owl and red fox. A water vole provides about ten times the protein of its cousin the field vole which is probably much better known to many of us. And this protein is provided by the vole through the vegetation which it consumes, thus helping to manage and conserve the surrounding flora. By the early 21st century the water vole was in danger of disappearing completely from Northumberland. A survey at the turn of the century revealed just a few surviving pockets, none in the Kielder Forest area.

So, a group of concerned naturalists (not naturists – this lot keep their clothes on) put together a plan for the re-introduction of the water vole in Northumberland. The chosen area was Kielder Forest. Here most of the land was under the ownership of one key player, the Forestry Commission. (now Forestry England unless you're reading this in a few years from now, by which time it probably has a new name). This made it relatively easy to monitor for mink, survey and plan for release sites. A partnership of Northumberland Wildlife Trust, Tyne Rivers Trust and Forestry England submitted a bid for funding from the National Lottery Heritage Fund – and it was successful! Initial funding was given to conduct surveys and to monitor for the presence of mink to ensure that the area was suitable for water vole release, and that any released voles wouldn't immediately be predated by them. Herons, on the other hand might get a free meal.

Chapter 2

Neville the Water Vole

"Beyond the Wild Wood comes the Wild World" said Ratty. "And that's something that doesn't matter, either to you or me. I've never been there, and I'm never going, nor you either, if you've got any sense at all. There's nothing – absolutely nothing - half so much worth doing as messing about in boats." ….. and then off he went to Devon!

(Kenneth Grahame: *Wind in the Willows*)

The Water Vole: (*Arvicola amphibius/terrestris*)
Until quite recently the water vole was known as *Arvicola terrestris* but then it was decided to change this to the current *Arvicola amphibius*. A bit ironic because at the same time we were beginning to gather evidence that this versatile little mammal could thrive perfectly well away from water courses as it does in parts of eastern Europe and, as we were about to discover, Glasgow!

Although in captivity water voles may live for two to three years, in the wild they are lucky to make it through the first year, with an average life span of only five to six months. It's pretty tough out there. Young born toward the end of the breeding season are unlikely to make it through the cold and scarcity of food in their first winter. Those born earlier in the year may have formed a significant part of the diet of their natural predators such as heron and stoat, as well as *Homo sapiens*, his dogs and the American mink. It is fortunate then that those females who do survive through a full breeding season may have produced between 20 and 40 offspring. With a survival rate through the winter of only 20% they'll all be needed. If Neville had been aware of these odds, would he have been looking forward to his new home in the north quite so much. Would it have been better to stay with Derek and enjoy life in the stud?

In appearance the water vole is a little similar to the brown rat but on closer inspection it is quite different. Water voles have rounded noses, deep brown to black fur, chubby faces and short fuzzy ears. The tail is about half the length of the body, unlike the much longer tail of the rat. Water vole feet, tails and ears are covered in hair, whereas in the rat these are all hairless. Water voles are also somewhat smaller than brown rats, although there will be quite a bit of overlap depending on the age and sex of the individual. A full-grown male water vole might be 20+cm in length (plus that tail of about 10/12cm) and weigh in at 390g (almost a pound). But most are smaller with an average species weight of 140g. In contrast the brown rat can grow up to 28cm, with a tail almost as long again and it may weigh up to 500g. The field vole on the other hand will only achieve a weight of 40g with a body around 10cm long and a short tail.

Like many rodents, water voles are prolific breeders. They need to be. The mating period lasts from March through to late autumn with the female gestation period being just 21 days. Up to eight naked kits are born, each weighing just 10 grams. Within three days their eyes are open and within three weeks they're fully weaned and out foraging for themselves. The females born in the first couple of litters will be ready to mate and produce offspring later that season. And mum will be ready to carry another brood just six weeks after conceiving the last lot! Not much chance of empty nesting here. A champion mum could be producing up to a mammoth family of 40 in one season! Highly unlikely though. First, she has to survive for more than the average five months and then the number of kits in each litter will vary, with four being much more likely than eight.

The colour of the fur on our voles is interesting. Whilst all European voles are recognised as the same species there are some small genetic differences between the voles found north of a line roughly between the Humber and the Mersey estuaries and those to the south. Those to the south may be slightly larger, although this may be down to a richer diet rather than genes. And northern voles tend to have a darker fur, many of them being almost black like Neville and his dad, whilst the southern vole is a dark chestnut on top and slightly paler below. One theory for this difference is that the southern voles arrived a little earlier, coming up from the region of what is now known as France, with their northern cousins crossing later from more northerly territories. As they have adapted to a slightly harsher environment, it has been thought best to breed from voles taken from the more northerly areas for release in Up-North and vice versa. So, our releasees have all been bred from voles taken in areas including the Trossachs, the North Pennines and the North Yorkshire Moors. And we hope that being brought up for the first few months of their lives in the pampered environment of Devon hasn't diminished their survival skills and northern sense of humour - 'cos they're going to need it. I'm sure Derek's tough regime in Devon will ensure that they would all do well in *Survivors*. (Check your TV schedule if you're unsure of what that is.)

So, when they're not in Devon dining on cream teas, what do water voles eat? Their main diet consists of grass and other herbaceous plants, but they will also dine on fruits, bulbs, roots and buds. In a Radio 4 programme in the late 1990s Rob Strachan quotes the example of a Hampshire farmer who accidentally exposed a water vole burrow system which contained a hundredweight of his prized potatoes! Whilst voles spend the spring and summer months grazing outside, in the autumn they will begin to store whatever they can find to see them through the winter. Water voles are seen much less often in the winter, partly because many of them have not survived but also because they spend longer underground. They will be eating from their larder or accessing the roots of plants via their burrow systems. In milder weather they will venture above ground for a while to find food but fewer sightings are reported. Well, it's dark most of the time, isn't it?

"Beavers typically get all the glory when it comes to building ecosystems, but water voles also play an important part in shaping Scottish wetlands. Though not as well known, these small but mighty creatures are eco-system engineers, positively increasing biodiversity and helping plants grow"
(Katy Anderson, Forestry & Land Scotland)

Water voles help to shape our land and encourage biodiversity in several ways. Their large front teeth continue to grow throughout their short lives, and these are used as their main tool for digging. Their extensive burrow systems involve the disturbance and movement of large amounts of soil. This helps bring nutrients to the surface thus encouraging vegetation to grow. And once it has grown, they can tuck in. More than 200 different plants have been recorded in the diet of the water vole, with thick grass being a particular favourite. Their grazing helps to control the growth of taller vegetation, thus encouraging wildflowers and native grasses to flourish.

As we've seen so far, lots of predators like to eat water voles. So, one assumes they are quite tasty. I can't find any culinary references to our water voles, although I'm sure there must be a Mary Berry or Nigella Lawson recipe somewhere. However, according to Wikipedia, the closely related southwestern water vole *(Arvicola sapidus)* was once a key ingredient in the Valencian paella. So, if you were in that part of Spain and thought it tasted of rabbit - who knows? Maybe the Italians have their own version. Anyone come across Spaghetti Arvicola? And do the Austrians like Vola Schnitzel? Anyone for Kelly's Bellingham Pie?

In spite of their prolific breeding habits, the population of water voles in the UK and throughout Europe has been declining rapidly. Pre-1960 it was estimated that there would have been a population of around eight million individuals. By 1990 a survey estimated that this had fallen to 2.3 million and by 2004 it was down to around 250,000 and still falling. The water vole is believed to be the UK's fastest declining mammal. Why? We have already mentioned the catastrophic impact that the release of American mink into the environment had in the 1990s, and which continues in many areas today. But other, probably equally significant causes relate to agriculture, forestry, water management and urban development. In none of these cases did anyone set out with the intention of harming these creatures. But our seemingly insatiable demand for more food, water, housing, timber etc. has resulted in the destruction, or if you like, change of land use, in those habitats once populated by the water vole. Farmers and foresters utilised all of the land available for growing their crops or grazing their livestock. Many water courses were straightened and dredged, and natural vegetation replaced with embankments and new crops. More and more land was taken for building and infrastructure.

By 2008 the UK government recognised the severity of the problem and introduced legal protection for water voles, making it an offence to take water voles from their natural habitat without a licence from Natural England, or to disturb, damage or obstruct their breeding places. This has had some beneficial impact on changing land use practices in some areas, such as not ploughing every bit of land down to the edges of watercourses where water voles might have their burrows and forage for food. But this has not been universal, and I could cite one example of a farm very close to home where every inch of land is utilised for crops and water courses, and hedgerows strictly managed so that yields are maximised. And I don't think you'll find many examples of perpetrators being prosecuted for this. And whilst regulations may cause some inconvenience to property developers, causing them to have environmental impact surveys undertaken and translocation plans put in place for disturbed populations of voles - or newts, or bats, or owls etc. - there is little evidence that these disturbed populations have thrived in their new homes. It seems that so long as the boxes are ticked few people really care about evaluating the outcomes. Whatever the case, there is no sign yet that water vole populations are recovering.

There have been a number of attempts around the country to protect and to re-introduce water voles in the Trossachs, in the North Yorkshire Moors, in Hampshire and Gloucestershire and recently in Cumbria and here in Northumberland with the largest-yet reintroduction programme. And we can rejoice in seeing these beautiful and essential components of a healthy ecosystem returning. And we can congratulate all of those dedicated people involved. And yet, to a degree it still feels like the boy with his finger in the dyke. (No jokes here about the holes being made by voles - this is serious.) Much more radical action is needed on a national scale. (Whoops! Sounds like I've been listening to too many woke lectures from Chris Packham and David Attenborough.) Both heroes.

A reintroduced vole (c) Joel Ireland

What was that I was saying earlier about Glasgow? Oh yes. Early in our project we were hearing rumours about a water vole population which was thriving, largely away from water courses, in the eastern suburbs of Glasgow. Best go up and have a look. We might learn something. So Graham and Kelly organised a trip for a group of staff and volunteers from NWT.

Conventional wisdom has been that water voles need to live close to water, just like Ratty in Wind *in the Willows*. But in Glasgow they seem to have adapted to a more urban environment. In such urban areas water courses have often been diverted underground or encased in concrete channels. Not very easy to burrow into these banks. The population came to light in 2008 when residents in the East End of Glasgow called the Environmental Health office complaining about the number of rats in their gardens and parks. However, when council experts attended, they got something of a surprise. The animals in question weren't rats at all. They were water voles. And more than a kilometre from any open water.

The council's biodiversity team knew that water voles existed along some of the city's waterways. They decided to survey areas away from these riparian corridors and were surprised to find water vole populations living in a wide variety of habitats.

When we visited, we were met and guided around the area by a member of staff from Glasgow University. Once alerted to the presence of water voles in unusual situations, the university had become interested and began scientific studies of these animals. The first site we visited was an area of open grassland situated between a council housing estate and the M8 motorway. It took us very little time to begin finding signs of burrows, latrines and feeding sites both within the grassland and along the M8 embankment. I hope these voles have good road traffic sense. And as Sue and I were ferreting (probably not an appropriate term in this context) through the long grass, we had a more typical urban experience. As we looked up, we saw two rather large, heavily tattooed gentlemen approaching from within the estate. We had been spotted.

It may seem stereotypical but one of these gentlemen had a can of Irn Bru in his hand. Yes, they were heading in our direction and so I casually slipped behind Sue. I won't attempt a Glaswegian accent, even though my sister-in-law was from the Gorbals. I never really got to grips with what she said to me through the haze of smoke and alcohol. Anyway, they had come for a chat. Were they upset at this intrusion into their 'hood or concerned that our blue NWT clothing might be linked to the polis? "Are you looking for our wee voles?", one of them asked. "Beautiful wee things, aren't they?" We chatted for a while and then they wandered off. I emerged from behind Sue. It was clear that the locals were very proud and very fond of their voles. Good news for their future, I hope. Both locals and voles.

Later we visited a public park where again there were plenty of signs of voles. And finally, the site of a primary school set within a public open space with a small playground and surrounded by high-rise flats, shops and major roads. No place for a vole you'd think, especially considering the number of dog walkers around. But no. The council were taking great care to ensure that there were substantial areas of long grass left unmown around the perimeters. Sure enough, in these areas burrows and latrines abounded. There was obviously a healthy population of voles, and some colleagues were lucky enough to see a few individuals popping out of their burrows. I wasn't jealous, honest.

Research led by Glasgow University has shown that in the city, the voles are doing better in these grassland areas than they are along the waterways, with some very high population densities. These grassland voles seem to have adapted by spending more of their time underground than their riverside cousins.

What a treat to visit these sites and to learn how Glasgow City Council and the university are working to protect these voles, and to extend and improve the habitats which encourage them. Lots of thanks to them for welcoming us on our visit to Glasgow and for the example they are setting for authorities all over the country. Look after what you've got. I wonder if Neville had some Glaswegian blood in him. Quite possible because the voles released in the Trossachs had been translocated from similar areas of Glasgow.

You might think the existence of these "fossorial" * voles has little relevance to our project in the remote uplands of Kielder Forest. But I think not. One of the problems we have had in assessing the success of our Restoring Ratty project has been the difficulties presented by the landscape and climate of the forest area. When trying to survey the areas where voles have been released, or we believe may have occupied, we have often had issues with accessing the sites and surveying along them. More of this later in the section on surveys. However, we have come to wonder whether some of our release sites may have encouraged the voles to set up home in the long vegetation away from the immediate surroundings of the streams where they can experience quite violent extremes of streamflow.

Interestingly just yesterday (November 2023) I was helping a friend to plant an area he owns in Weardale with Scots pine. I asked him if there were water voles living around the stream which runs through his land. His answer was revealing. There had been a healthy population until last year when a violent rainstorm led to the stream flooding and washing away large areas of the bank where the voles had their burrows. He hasn't seen a water vole on his land since. But there are some downstream where they had not been seen previously. Good evidence that these voles are adaptable and can cope with quite catastrophic damage to their home environment by moving on and finding somewhere more attractive. I believe it is well known that vole populations do move territories when conditions suggest they need to.

Note: "Fossorial" refers to living in burrows. Most water voles are fossorial to some extent, although in some areas they build nests using the long vegetation which they prefer. But the Glasgow voles are entirely burrow-dwelling and spend longer underground. Some of us became a bit more fossorial during lockdown.

Chapter 3

Neville's Nemesis

The Mink and Other Invasives

American mink (Neovison neovison) (C) Tom Hibbert

So, vole good, mink bad? Is it as simple as that? We'll leave Neville out of this poll. He may be biased. I find public attitudes, à la vox pops, to be very interesting. And this can also apply to many people in the conservation/rewilding community. There is nothing intrinsically evil about an American mink, a grey squirrel, signal crayfish or Himalayan balsam. And yet these are often referred to as "vermin" and described in language which makes them appear abhorrent. People may speak of them in tones which imply hatred. But they are just natural creatures or plants, often quite beautiful or impressive. They just find themselves in the wrong place through no fault of their own. Trying to get by. Often very successfully because the host eco-system isn't adjusted for their presence. If there is a fault here, whose is it? It's usually us. *Homo sapiens*. We have interfered with the natural world so comprehensively and destructively that there is no longer a balance. And species introduced to inappropriate environments can cause havoc. Without any apex predators red deer have totally altered the landscape of the Scottish Highlands, and they're not even foreign! The brown rat all but wiped-out nesting seabird colonies on islands as diverse as Lundy in the Bristol Channel and South Georgia in the South Atlantic.

So there is a problem here. And maybe we, who have caused the destruction, need to be the ones to address it. This may be painful and regrettable in many instances, and we have to make decisions about where and when to intervene. But let's not blame the American mink for being brought here to be bred for its fur and then released to bring mayhem when it was no longer profitable. We don't hold the moral high ground here and shouldn't feel triumphant when we manage to control the problem by killing it. Perhaps we should be asking for forgiveness as we do it.

Well. That was a bit of a rant so let's focus on the American mink. I'll just call it mink from now on

Paw print of American Mink   *Mink Poo! Very smelly.*

The mink is a member of the mustelid family. In the UK native mustelids include otter, stoat, weasel, pine marten and polecat. In addition, we have feral ferrets (a domesticated form of polecat) and, since the 1920s we have a sizeable population of mink. Like all mustelids the mink is just about exclusively carnivorous and will eat birds, fish, reptiles and small mammals, including our water vole. What makes it particularly hazardous for the water voles is that the mink is semi-aquatic like the otter. So, whenever a mink enters the territory of water voles it can cause havoc. There is little chance of escape because the smaller female mink is able to enter the burrow system and will kill any voles unlucky enough to be at home.

The mink is about three times the size of a water vole, reaching a length of up to 65cm. and a kilogram in weight. Compared to the 20cm and 390g of the largest water vole. The mink has partially webbed feet and a water-repellent coat like the otter and so is well suited to life along a waterway or on the coast. It has been suggested that the resurgence of the otter population in recent years is good news for the voles because the otter will not tolerate mink on its territory and will kill or drive off the offender. However, there is some evidence of otter and mink co-existing along some waterways and the most likely scenario is that the otters will drive mink away but not permanently. When the otter moves on mink may return. And the wary vole must always remember that otters will eat them too. It's just that otters can't get into the burrow and that makes life a bit safer. And simply getting rid of mink isn't the end of the story. We still have to face the facts that modern agricultural practices, urban development and an imbalance in our eco-system and its food chains will be significant barriers to a recovery of the water vole population.

As discussed earlier, mink are here because of the fur trade in the twentieth century. The first mink farms were established in the 1920s and by the 1950s a wild population had established itself, the base of this population being a few animals which had escaped or been released. These escapees were probably already having a detrimental effect on native wildlife along the waterways which they inhabited, but there was little recording or surveying done to measure this impact. The situation was made considerably worse by the collapse of the fur industry in the 1990s. Effective campaigning by animal rights activists and associated groups led to a decline in fur sales, although faux fur remained popular, and this led to the production of mock fur made from products of the petrochemical industry. More plastic for the environment. You can't win, can you?

Anyway, most mink farms closed down. The most responsible disposed of their livestock humanely or sold it on to farms based in Europe. But there were also reports of farms simply releasing the animals to fend for themselves, and of animal rights groups liberating the mink. Whatever the cause, by the end of the century a substantial population was established throughout the UK with the greatest concentrations being in the south of England and in the north-east and eastern Scotland. Few areas escaped, a few areas on the west coast of Scotland, some of the Hebridean islands, Orkney and Shetland, the Isle of Man, Anglesey and the Isle of Wight. What were we going to do now? Doing nothing would mean the threat of extinction for water voles and significant damage to other wildlife.

Can we get rid of the mink?
So, is it possible to eradicate mink in the British Isles? There is hope but it would take far more investment than has been forthcoming to date. In 2022 Tony Martin of Dundee University came to Rainham Meadows Nature Reserve to talk to staff and volunteers representing Northumberland, Durham and Tees Valley Wildlife Trusts and members of the Naturally Native team. Naturally Native was a three-year-funded project aimed at restoring water voles in the north east largely through habitat restoration and mink eradication rather than through releases of voles. Between 2022 and 2023 project staff, including Northumberland's Emily Marshall, deployed baited humane traps along the riparian corridors associated with the rivers Tyne, Wear and Tees. They have had some success. The greatest numbers of mink have been caught along the Tees where they seemed to be most numerous. In Northumberland Emily's catches have been much lower. Good news, as it suggests the threat of mink predation is going to be less in our release areas and their surroundings. But no room for complacency as mink are still being trapped, most recently on the Tarset Burn which lies just below the Kielder Dam. And just as the project might seem to be being effective, the funding runs out. Typical of these short-term funding projects. When will we learn? Whilst a funding bid is being prepared to continue and expand the great work done by the Naturally Native staff, by the time it is agreed, if at all, the expert staff will have moved on and the mink will have had time to breed up again.

Tony Martin's talk was particularly pointed and well received. Neville's a big fan. Tony had previously been the project manager responsible for the eradication of invasive rodents: rats and mice, which had been decimating the seabird colonies on the island of South Georgia in the South Atlantic. Using the experience gained there, Tony was now working with the University of Cambridge and local wildlife trusts on a project to eradicate mink in East Anglia. The project was known as Waterlife Recovery East. Having managed to attract sufficient funding, a relatively small team has had quite dramatic success so far. The project has concentrated almost exclusively on the use of "smart" traps which use up-to-date technology to alert the centre when a trap is triggered. This has allowed the team to deploy a large number of traps, housed in mink rafts. The strategy has been to concentrate the traps in areas where local evidence suggests the presence of a number of mink. As the frequency of captures declines in this core area, the traps can be moved to another core area or to widen the protected zone. The initial aim to virtually eradicate mink in most of Norfolk and Suffolk was achieved in just a few years, with a buffer zone of some 60 kms then monitored and trapped to guard against repopulation. In 2023 it was estimated that a mink population of approximately 10,000 had been reduced to fewer than 1,000, in just 3 years. So it seems that it can be done if sufficient resources are deployed. And if this were done over the whole island, it would be of great benefit to our native species and it would save much more money and effort in the future.

One key reason for the success of the team lay in the bait which was used to attract mink into the traps. And Tony delighted in not only telling us about this but also demonstrating how the bait was sourced. Look away now and hold your nose if you're of a sensitive disposition. The bait in question was taken from the anal scent gland of the mink which had been trapped and dispatched. A number of deceased and frozen mink corpses had been brought along by the Naturally Native team. After Tony demonstrated the technique volunteers were invited to practise the dissection of the mink and the removal of the scent gland. Suffice it to say that mink may be attracted to this smell, but it is unlikely to make it as a perfume present for Xmas. If you are thinking of establishing a close relationship with anyone engaged in mink trapping, you may wish to enquire as to whether they are in the habit of using this particular bait and then think again.

On a more serious note, Waterlife Recovery East has now become the Waterlife Recovery Trust and is applying for significant funding to allow it to continue to expand its core area so that it eventually covers the whole of the UK, and we are rid of this unfortunate invader. And developments in the Hebrides support the view that this should be possible.

In 1969 the first mink was caught on the Isle of Lewis and by 2001 they had spread throughout the main islands as far south as South Uist. Breeding populations of sea birds and ground nesting birds were severely depleted and particularly noticeable amongst these were Arctic and common terns, black and red throated divers, dunlin, corncrake, ringed plover and dipper. Some iconic species which contribute strongly to the unique nature of these fabulous islands. The Outer Hebrides are one of my favourite places to visit. Fabulous wildlife, great scenery, wildflowers galore in the summer months on the machair and a feeling of being somewhere quite unique. But beware. If your idea of a great holiday includes sun loungers and Bacardi Breezers, you need to accept that this isn't possible every day out here, and you'd be advised to pack some warm clothing and waterproofs for those breezy days of another type.

Anyway, mink are definitely not welcome on the islands. So Scottish Natural Heritage applied for and received sufficient funding from the EU Life programme to employ a team of rangers to tackle the problem. Trapping began in 2001 and covered the area from the Uists and Benbecula across to Harris and as far north as the Butt of Lewis. Thanks to the sustained efforts of the staff by 2013 well over 2,000 mink had been trapped and dispatched. The size of the trapping team was reduced and in 2016 only seven mink were caught, and in 2018 only two non-breeding individuals. Whilst staff will need to remain vigilant, we can be reasonably confident that mink are no longer a threat. And bird colonies are recovering strongly.

Other Invasives

In 2018 I read a quite challenging book by science writer Fred Pearce. It was called *The New Wild* and it offered an interesting outlook, backed up with examples and facts. In the book, Fred argues that there is no such thing as a pristine and entirely "native" natural environment. Nowhere on the planet remains the same for long periods of time. Climate change has always occurred, although generally at a less alarming rate than now. In addition, wildfires, volcanoes, earthquakes, flooding etc. all bring about changes to the natural environment which provide threats and opportunities for the local flora and fauna. Some species will decline whilst others multiply and some species new to the area may move in. Often this is a gradual process, at other times swift and dramatic. But are these changes "wrong" or unnatural? No. With or without our interference, new or invasive species will move into an area. Fred quotes a number of examples on a global scale where this has significantly added to the biodiversity in the area with very few species being adversely affected. He also suggests that we can become too alarmist about some species and gives the example of Japanese knotweed. Here the evidence suggests that when this plant has "escaped" from its previous location, probably someone's garden, it will generally only spread into vacant areas such as brownfield sites and along railway lines and rarely out-competes indigenous plants. I think Fred makes some valid points here and the main thing I take away from his book is the thought that we need to look carefully at each individual case before we rush to action. On the other hand, sometimes we need to react more quickly if we are to prevent significant damage. Just look at the impact of mammals on the wildlife of New Zealand or the mink in the Outer Hebrides. I can't, therefore go all the way with Fred, and suggest that we should stand back and let nature take care of itself, adapting as it will eventually, and achieving at length a new balance. We have upset the balance too much for this I think and stand to lose too much if we don't act to give nature a hand.

Chapter 4

Friends of Neville

Robin Bailey at Dummy's Hole. Graham and Tom relax in the background.

The Volunteer

Having decided that there was a good reason for attempting to re-introduce the water vole, and that the mink were a significant threat to the whole enterprise, now we had to get on with it. And to do this a workforce would be needed. Who would they be and where would they come from? We had the equivalent of a full-time officer in the partnership of Kelly and Graham but there's only so much one person can do. A reasonably dedicated group of volunteers would be needed. They would need to be able to drive and navigate their way around the extensive Kielder Forest with only an OS map to guide them. No signposts or traffic lights, no white lines or pedestrian crossings. But there is a notional speed limit. They would also have to learn the mechanics of mink raft monitoring and surveying. It was initially hoped that these volunteers would come from the immediate surroundings of Kielder but this turned out to be not possible. There simply aren't enough people in the area. So the net had to be spread wider, and I was caught in it, together with several others from various parts of Northumberland and Newcastle. We all have our own reasons and motivations for getting involved in volunteering of any sort and I won't attempt to explain them here. I can only speak for myself.

After 45 years working in education as a comprehensive school teacher of geography and humanities, school leader, local authority adviser and school inspector, I was looking forward to the next phase of life and what I wanted it to be. Retirement for me wasn't about doing less, it was about doing something different. It certainly wouldn't be to do with education. Whilst I still enjoyed visiting schools, talking to pupils and staff and, I hope, offering some support and useful advice, I had seriously fallen out with the work of Ofsted and the local authority. No, I was looking for something to help me grow in other directions. I wanted to be outside, doing something practical and worthwhile. And I wanted to learn more about the natural world. I turned to Northumberland Wildlife Trust for succour. And I got it in bucketloads. I hadn't met Neville yet, but I must have had some sort of premonition. It was meant to be.

The first task I set myself was finding out how to volunteer with NWT. Easy enough you'd think but back in 2010 this involved attending an induction session at the Trust's HQ in Newcastle. This is situated within the grounds of an NHS hospital which specialises in psychiatric disorders. Subsequent events may suggest that this was appropriate and finding the building on a dark winter's night didn't help with my state of mind. Nevertheless, I eventually arrived after driving around the local housing estates for a while. I was a little bit late but given a warm welcome and soon signed up for my first task. This was vaguely described as "site maintenance", a term I came to know well and which could mean any one of many inviting activities. It was to be at Holywell Pond. The pond bit might have been a warning. The pond in question is quite large and the result of subsidence caused by coal mining in the south east of the county. The task turned out to be assisting with the installation of a new fence which needed to extend out into the shallow waters of the said pond in order to prevent grazing livestock from escaping from the pasture alongside the pond. It was a cold day. Sleet was blowing across the exposed site. The work of loading materials and carrying them onto site under the instruction of our leader, whom I shall refer to as "Geoff" (because that's his name), helped to keep us warm. I had prepared for the day with sufficient warm and waterproof clothing, or so I thought. As I gained some experience of these days with Geoff, I realised I needed several more layers. This realisation came about as I was asked to take a pole out into the shallow waters of the rather cold lake so that a bearing could be taken to ensure that the fence was constructed in a straight line. With water lapping around the top of my wellies and a brisk north-easterly driving the sleet into my face, I struggled to keep the pole straight. We couldn't have a wonky fence on my first task, could we? As Geoff shouted, "left a bit, bit further, no more to the right, keep it straight", I reflected on how positive this step into the future might become. It was probably only 20 minutes or so, but it seemed like several hours. This helped me to understand that I needed a better pair of wellies. Not a particularly positive first task you might think. But I quite enjoyed myself in a masochistic sort of way. I felt refreshed in mind and body. But a bit weatherbeaten. And the group of people who were involved was encouraging and turned out to be characteristic of all of my time with the trust. People from all types of backgrounds and ages with varying degrees of skill and knowledge. But a shared interest in nature and in doing something worthwhile.

Friendly but rarely intrusive. A pretty common set of values, with the odd exception. You do wonder about the odd individuals who keep asking which animals and birds it is OK to shoot. They don't tend to last long. Not that we've "got rid" of them of course. There were three Geoffs altogether on that first day, and since then I have tended to think of NWT staff and volunteers as a group of Geoffs, even though I haven't encountered many extras since then. The task suggested there was some purpose to be had and some new skills to learn. I'm not sure standing still and holding a pole whilst shivering violently is a very advanced skill but it would do for a start. And there had been encouraging talk of wildlife and other reserves that could be visited. And on the way home in the van, Morris conducted an enjoyable quiz to keep everyone's' spirits up, although I think those on the back seats were asleep.

Would I sign up for more? Some people don't. Some think again about what they want in life. Others ask if there are any volunteer tasks to be had in a nice warm office. But I went for it. There followed many enjoyable days out in the more and less remote parts of Northumberland; planting trees, laying boardwalks, building steps, pulling up thistles and Himalayan balsam, mending fences and sometimes just doing nice gentle surveys on sunny days. From the high fells of Whitelee Moor to the urban delights of Dougie's Pond, I began to learn about some of the less well-known parts of the county. And what was I getting out of this? Lots is written and spoken about the health and wellbeing impacts of both volunteering and being out in nature. Let me try to put it into my own words.

Benefit 1. Giving a purpose to life. This would apply to all forms of volunteering whether in or outdoors and that is the feeling of doing something worthwhile. For me that has largely been about giving nature a hand and doing my minuscule bit to recompense the natural world for all of the harm we have done and continue to do as a species. But it can be other things too. For a year I volunteered as a delivery driver for Fareshare. This fantastic organisation engages a large number of volunteers in its warehouses and delivery networks, collecting in donations of food from farms, supermarkets, the food production industry and others and delivering these to those in need via food banks and other charitable organisations. It tells you something about people's tastes too. I remember one day having cartons of frozen pasties to drop off with each delivery. The first two clients turned them down. Couldn't use them. Strange I thought. So, when client three said the same I asked why. It turned out that each week they got a free delivery of fresh pasties and sausage rolls from a well-known baker called "G****s". Sorry can't advertise here. Their customers wouldn't eat any other. So well done to that baker for making sure that their surplus fresh food didn't get wasted but went to a very good cause. I trust they're still doing it. This different type of voluntary work again gave me a real sense of purpose. Once more the feeling that my seemingly tiny contribution can be a part of something much bigger and desperately needed in our rather imbalanced society. Unfortunately, after a year with Fareshare my back gave in and I had to take a break from lifting those heavy crates laden with stones of potatoes or cans of beans. (For you youngsters a "stone" being an imperial weight equivalent to several kilograms rather than a scam where someone replaces real spuds with bricks.)

In contrast I could mention the character I came across in my local newsagent a couple of years ago. He shuffled in looking tired and dispirited and bought his newspaper and a loaf of bread. When the proprietor asked how he was finding his new retirement that he had been looking forward to, his response was along the lines of …. "Well, it's all right I suppose. In the morning, I get up when I like and have a cup of tea. Then I'll maybe have a bit of breakfast. Then I'll come down for the paper, go home and have a cup of tea. I'll read the paper and do the crossword and have a cup of tea. It'll soon be time for lunch. Then I'll watch a bit of telly and have a cup of……" You guessed it. This went on for the rest of his day.

When I asked whether he had any hobbies or pastimes he replied, "not really, but I like watching the football". It would drive me up the wall!

Benefit 2. Fresh air. Sounds simple but it is amazing how much difference this makes to my mood and clarity of thought. Whatever the weather or time of year, just getting out of the house or the car and standing in clean fresh air seems to cleanse my being. It might be a stroll with a friend or on my own. Or it might often be on an NWT task. Having chosen a task, signed up and committed myself to it, I'll do my utmost to be there. It might seem a drag having to rise in the dark on a cold winter's morning like today but once I'm out there I love it. Whether it's a small reserve near the city or one of our larger and wilder reserves like Whitelee Moor on the Scottish border I'm up for it. But usually, I'll have chosen the latter only if my back is up to the task involved. Peter's steps at Northumberlandia and Geoff's boardwalk at Carter Bar having been a major contribution to my failing back. Can't give Fareshare all the blame.

Benefit 3. Nature therapy. Sitting on the bank of the Scaup Burn in Kielder Forest and enjoying the companionship of a group of like-minded colleague volunteers. Sometimes chatting and putting the world to rights. Discussing how the government, NWT or anyone else, could do things much better if they just listened to us. But often just listening to the stream bubbling past over the boulders with the sand martins and buzzards flying overhead. Sue saw a golden eagle once, according to local folklore. By local I mean the gang in the van. Out here the worries of normal - or should it be abnormal - life seem much less significant. It's almost as if one is being absorbed by the landscape and the natural world around. Places like this are so special. And increasingly rare. I can feel my body and my mind relaxing. And then the call of the wild - "Come on, back in the van, time to get on with it". "It" could be one of many things. Planting trees, bashing bracken, checking our mink rafts. The positive feelings don't go away, it just gets more physical. Great days.

Benefit 4. The Green Gym. That's what my friend John calls it when he wants to recruit a few volunteers for a bit of work on his very own bit of land at Liddells in the Tyne Valley. And it's the same thing when out with the Wildlife Trust. Out in the open air completing a physical task which has some benefit for nature and for others. Hard, or hard as you want to make it, physical work which makes the blood flow and the muscles strain a bit. And in the open air. Far better than a hot, sweaty gym with some awful music playing in the background whilst some posers look around to check that you've noticed their abs. Well, some people prefer that.

Benefit 5. Learning. There is so much we don't know. And when we move into a new sphere of life and activity there is so much we can learn. I thought joining the NWT would really help me to gain much needed knowledge about the natural world, trees, flowers, insects, birds and mammals. And to be fair it has helped me to gain some knowledge about all of these. But for a while I thought I was learning much more about how to get rid of things that weren't wanted - thistles, bracken, bramble etc. In the wrong place all of these can be detrimental to other native species. So, learning about habitats and bio-diversity. Finding hidden parts of the county which I would never have visited otherwise. And learning new practical skills such as the use of the "lazy dog" and the brush cutter. How to plant trees, how to fell unwanted trees. Constructing boardwalks and steps, mending fences. Even a bit of sheep wrangling. The list goes on. After years of "white collar" activity it has been refreshing to learn new skills and develop more confidence in a new area of life. Some of it has felt like learning a new language.

Benefit 6. Psychological welfare of family members. I can't speak for others, but my wife Cath would suffer serious psychological stress if I were at home all of the time. Well, that's what she tells me. One of the dangers of retirement, I think. Dreaming of doing nothing all day and spending one's life cruising (you can choose your own meaning here) might seem appealing when you're up to your eyes with work but leaping from 60-hour weeks to zero hours is going to be a shock. My first few months of retirement were very relaxing. Getting up with the sun, planning each day as it comes, drifting through the weeks. That's a holiday. For me it's not a way of life. For me "retirement" needed to mean shifting from one way of life into another, but equally fulfilling one. I remember reading one noted philosopher - and I can't recall which - suggesting that the key to a happy life is "knowing what you're doing tomorrow". I think I understand what he meant and I agree to a certain extent. Just as long as what it is you'll be doing will bring you a sense of pleasure or fulfilment.

Benefit 7. Social. Meeting new people from all sorts of backgrounds and with so many varied opinions can be quite challenging. I am quite a shy person I suppose. Not great at casual social situations and small talk. It would be easy for me to sink into a world where my social contacts were limited to a few close friends and family. And this can bring its own stresses and conflicts. So having a reason to get out there and have the shared purpose of the task to bring a disparate group together has great benefit for me. And I have met so many people during my now 14 years with NWT. Some of them, staff and volunteers I would now think of as friends, and I hope one or two of them might reciprocate. No names required here. And there have been very few that I wouldn't work happily alongside. Just a couple but I won't go into that now. I couldn't afford the legal fees.

So, all in all a pretty good list of positives for me. Negatives? I'm not fond of midges and there were a couple of days in gale-force winds with driving rain when I've thought I should have stayed in bed. Oh, yes. On one occasion I stuck my hand into what I thought was a water vole burrow only to disturb a nest of wasps! Ouch.

OK, back to September 2014 and that first meeting to recruit volunteers for what was to become "Restoring Ratty". Why was I there? By now I had almost four years of experience with NWT. I had experienced the joys of the Whitelee Workout, the Briarwood Burnout, Border Mire-ing and Tony's Patch and so had a fair idea of what to expect on those. But this idea of a mammal restoration project sounded different and intriguing. Possibly what I had thought I might find. And I had worked with Kelly before. I wasn't alone of course. Those first sixteen soon dwindled to a core of about six enthusiasts with many more joining in for the short, medium or long term over the ten years since.

Chapter 5

Neville's New Home

Kielder Forest and Reservoir: (inc. Wildwood, Osprey Watch, Bakethin etc)
Neville was born and raised on Dartmoor but he always knew he belonged in UpNorth where the winds blow strong and clean. So, when the chance came to join the expedition back to the homelands he jumped at the chance. But what would this new place be like?

Kielder Forest covers an area of over 650 square km (250 square miles) and nestles right up on the Scottish border. It's a pretty remote area nowadays although once it had its own railroad and was generally much busier. There were very few trees here 100 years ago. Now 75% of the area is covered by forest with smaller patches of rough pasture found within the designated area and the large artificial lake of Kielder Reservoir. Both forest and reservoir are the largest of their kind in Western Europe.

Part of Kielder Forest and the Reservoir from the Dark Sky Observatory

By 2014 surveys showed no evidence that water voles lived here any more although local residents report having seen them in abundance during their lifetime. Mink were seen occasionally but not thought to be numerous. And so, it was decided that this would be a good place to try for a reintroduction of the water vole. Funding had been found and volunteers recruited. But what sort of challenge would the forest present?

Before I started working with the Wildlife Trust my impression of Kielder Forest was based largely on the experience of driving past on the A68 en route to Edinburgh, or possibly Byrness first school. I had occasionally driven up through Bellingham to Kielder and knew the reservoir was there. In the distant past, 1974 in fact, I had set out to walk the Pennine Way in reverse. Most people set out from the southern extremity at Edale in Derbyshire but at the time I was living and working in Derby and decided it would make more sense to finish close to home and so set off for Scotland. On the third day my companion and I set off from Byrness heading for Bellingham and then Once Brewed on Hadrian's Wall. This entailed passing through the eastern edge of Kielder Forest. We soon entered the forest and had gone no more than a couple of miles when we were suddenly shocked by the emergence of several soldiers in full camouflage and blackened faces who leapt out in front of us with rifles raised. As you can imagine we were a bit perturbed. But we did survive as you can probably tell. It turned out these were members of 9 Para on an exercise. Their notional task was to intercept 2 enemy spies who had been dropped secretly in the Cheviot hills and were en route to Hadrian's Wall to assassinate the Prime Minister who was due there on a visit. Let me emphasise this was a training exercise with no link to reality at the time. Had it happened today there would be several recent PMs one might put forward as appropriate targets.

This group of paras had surmised that a good way for the spies to make their way south would be to team up with members of the opposite sex and pretend to be on a walking holiday. They were, therefore checking out any suspicious looking couples on the trail. I mean, do I look like a spy? Fortunately, we persuaded them of our innocence and were soon on our way. Unfortunately, I must have been spooked (get it?) by this event because the next day I fell and badly sprained my ankle. As a result of which the holiday was abandoned and we ended up in Portugal! What? Why? How? Here's why? On returning to Derby, we decided to make up for the disappointment by booking a package holiday in the sun so that I could rest the ankle. The only places available at the last minute turned out to be in Portugal. Not a bad choice. And the reason was because Portugal was in the throes of what turned out to be a peaceful revolution. The people had risen up against the dictator Salazar and the army had joined them. Images of tanks with flowers in their barrels and people hugging the soldiers were being shown on the TV. Nevertheless, most people had cancelled their holidays and there were lots of vacancies. We ended up in a large hotel in Estoril where only 20 of the 600 rooms were taken. We were outnumbered by the jubilant staff and had a wonderful week. Many thanks to those boys from 9 Para. I never did get around to walking the Pennine Way. Would I lie to you? This story is in fact true.

As a result of the above experiences, my image of Kielder Forest was of a huge uninterrupted block of conifers, a dark and forbidding place possibly inhabited by members of the armed forces. The truth turns out to be very different. Yes, there are many blocks of commercial forest, well over 180 million trees I'm told, but there are also pockets of pastureland belonging to the few remaining farms, a handful of still-occupied private houses, hidden valleys containing small areas of native woodland and heather-topped moorland above the tree line. At the very top of Kielder Burn lies the extensive Kielderhead nature reserve which adjoins NWT's Whitelee Moor nature reserve. And of course, we have Kielder Water itself and its surroundings and visitor centres. The more I've got to know the forest and its mosaic of habitats, the more I've got to love it and the days I've been privileged to work there. Still don't like the midges though.

If you had visited the area before 1920; unlikely I know, even for me; you would have found no forest and no lake. This was an area of rough grazing for sheep, and grouse shooting on the open moorland. You would have found the remains of numerous small coal pits and even an iron smelter at Lewisburn. But all this had gone. However, the railway which had been constructed in 1856 remained, but dwindled in importance and finally closed in 1958. You can still see the impressive viaduct on the edge of Kielder village, built to mirror the style of the Duke of Northumberland's shooting lodge nearby. But in 1920 great changes were about to commence. Following timber shortages during World War 1 the government established the Forestry Commission whose task it was to make Britain more self-sufficient in timber, especially for pit props at that time. Kielder Forest was established and planting began. The land was purchased by the state and remains in public ownership today under the management of what is now Forestry England. The imperative was to grow timber and many deep furrows were ploughed to create drier land for planting with deep ditches for drainage in-between. These ditches were to make our life extremely difficult when it came to travelling across these often-steep hillsides. And ploughing and planting extended right down to watercourses in the valleys, destroying suitable habitat for the water vole and changing the nature of the streams which became fast flowing and likely to destroy any stream-side burrows when in spate. None of this was intentional of course. At that time few people were aware of the fact that the UK was rapidly destroying its native flora and fauna. By the year 2000, 75% of the area had been planted up, mainly with Sitka spruce which copes well with the climate and terrain. And also with varying amounts of lodgepole pine, Douglas fir, larch and Scots pine.

Things changed in 1960 when the remit of the Forestry Commission was extended to include nature conservation and recreation. Forestry England (FE) is still a commercial enterprise producing around 500,000 cubic metres of timber a year. If you're driving around rural Northumberland, you're likely to come across some of this being transported down to the large pulp mill in the Tyne Valley. Watch how you go. These are large wagons on small roads and they're in a hurry. But in addition to producing timber, FE is now making major efforts to enhance the natural environment, and planting regimes have changed to cater for this and to encourage wildlife. Excellent examples of this include their partnerships with Northumberland Wildlife Trust in the Restoring Ratty project, and the Kielder Wildwood project which has been transforming one of the more remote valleys along the Scaup Burn.

And 1976 saw the construction of the largest man-made reservoir in western Europe, Kielder Water. Originally intended to supply water to the industries of Teesside - steel, shipbuilding and chemicals - this large body of water is now largely used for recreational purposes, although it also helps to control the flow of the North Tyne and so helps to mitigate against flooding further downstream. So now we have the Kielder Forest and Water Park which attracts thousands of visitors to the area. Some of these are encountered whilst monitoring and surveying in the area. It's usually good natured, although the odd mountain biker has been known to give our trusty Isuzu a hard stare as they squeeze past on the forest tracks.

There we have it. Water voles will soon be on their way, mink monitoring has begun and volunteers are trying to find their way around the forest. None have been lost so far. A few of us had a little previous, and concurrent experience with the forest through our involvement in other NWT activities.

A.   Northumbrian Water Reserves. For some time now NWT has been contracted by Northumbrian Water to maintain and develop its reserves which lay around its main reservoirs. These include Fontburn, Colt Crag, Carsington and Whittle Dene as well as those around Kielder Water. Each has its own unique character and wildlife interest. At Kielder the relevant sites were around Bakethin Reservoir, which lies at the north-west extremity of the main reservoir, separated from it by a weir, Leaplish Waterside and Falstone Moss. Until her appointment as what we affectionately called "The Ratty Czar", Kelly was employed to look after the Kielder reserves, and a small group of volunteers helped out with activities such as maintaining the red squirrel hide at Leaplish, strimming paths and grassland areas, tree planting, hedgerow management etc. Kielder Forest is one of the largest remaining havens for red squirrels in England. It was several of this group - volunteers not squirrels - who initially joined the Ratty team.

B.   Osprey Watch. Whilst it was Forestry England who established and maintained the series of nesting platforms which attracted the osprey to return to this remote part of England, Northumbrian Water in partnership with NWT set up an osprey viewpoint so that visitors and bird enthusiasts could have the opportunity to see these magnificent birds in the wild. Initially this was set up at the visitor centre at Leaplish. A remote camera was placed alongside Nest 1 so that live footage of the ospreys, their eggs and chicks could be seen at close hand. Telescopes were set up on a viewing platform and manned by volunteers on several days per week. Information boards gave visitors basic information and the volunteers were there to give further help. More recently the Osprey Watch site has been relocated to the Tower Knowe visitor centre and receives lots of interest every spring and summer. One year, 2011 I think, I joined this volunteer group, giving up a day a fortnight or so to help out. I found it wasn't really my cup of tea. Standing around in all weathers, chatting to visitors, supervising youngsters who would insist on moving the telescopes which had been set up so that they were focussed on the nest didn't do it for me. I was too restless. I think so many years in education may have given me ADHD! But it was interesting and the osprey story is fascinating.

The osprey is one of our largest birds of prey with a wingspan of up to six feet. Their diet consists entirely of fish hence their common name of the fish eagle. Not as big as our golden eagle but a bit bigger than a buzzard, it is a magnificent sight to see one of these birds diving for fish or flying back to its nest carrying a trout back to feed the family. Sue and I were privileged one day to witness this very process as we were driving along the forest tracks to check our next mink raft. The bird flew over the van and we slowed to a halt to watch it. And then we were rewarded by the sight of another adult rising from the trees to greet it. Probably the female. And it got even better as two further birds, this year's brood, also rose into the sky. All four birds circled the nest for a while, calling to one another until the male descended to the nest, fish in talons, to be quickly followed by its no doubt ravenous brood. What a treat. I'm not sure what Neville would have been thinking. Those are pretty threatening-looking birds. Not to worry Neville, they only eat fish.

The osprey had been extinct in England since 1840, and in Scotland by 1916, largely because of persecution by gamekeepers jealous of their fish stocks, and Victorian egg and skin collectors. We're wonderful, we humans. However, as persecution diminished ospreys began returning to Scotland from their breeding grounds in Scandinavia and bred for the first time in 1954 at Loch Garten. As the population grew ospreys were often seen overflying Kielder on their annual migrations to and from their wintering grounds in West Africa. To encourage them to stop over and nest here, Forestry England built a number of potential nesting platforms at the tops of some suitable trees. The age and homogeneous nature of a commercial forest doesn't provide a lot of suitable sites for a nest. And the new platforms brought success. In 2009 the first birds nested successfully on one of these platforms. Since then new nests have appeared in most years, so that by 2023 there were nine pairs of nesting ospreys on the water and several unattached birds in the area. And it's great news that a pair have set up a nest at Catcleugh Reservoir which lies at the head of Redesdale, just a short fly across the watershed from the North Tyne for an osprey. Even better news was that these birds had found a natural site for a nest and hadn't needed a prepared platform to tempt them.

The first birds return from Africa towards the end of March, a fact which brought me enormous pleasure on 24th March 2012. A small group of volunteers, including myself, Don and Kelly (she wasn't the Ratty Czar then, just Baroness Bakethin I think) were afloat in a small boat heading for Oystercatcher Island when a large bird was spotted bearing down on the boat from the lakeside. "Look it's a buzzard", exclaimed one of the crew. But it wasn't a buzzard. As the bird flew quite low overhead, we could see its striking white underside and its longer, more slender wings. We even got a good view of those long talons which it uses for "hooking" its fish. "Wow, it's an osprey", yelled the bosun and everyone jumped up to get a better view. It has to be said here that jumping up in a small boat, even in unison, is not recommended by the Health and Safety Executive or the Admiralty. I should know because my brother was in the Royal Navy. Anyway, with good fortune we all survived and glowing with pleasure we landed on the island and spent a very pleasant, warm and sunny spring day clearing the island of vegetation to expose the gravel which the oystercatchers like to build their nest upon.

C.   Kielder Wildwood. Just one more before we get back to Neville and his friends.

If you leave the NWT centre in Gosforth, Newcastle upon Tyne and drive for an hour in a north west direction you will eventually reach the small town of Bellingham. You will have driven along a variety of roads, some of them hilly and winding, and you might have had some great views of the surrounding countryside with rolling hills disappearing into the far distance. At the highest point in the drive, before you drop down to Bellingham you might have caught a glimpse of the Cheviot to the north and Cross Fell - highest point in the Pennine hills - to the west. But if you're driving you've probably missed these because it's wise to keep your eyes on the road to avoid timber wagons and Dutch tourists in their caravans and mobile homes. Best to watch out for the roe deer too. I was once in collision with a large one on the A68 as it sailed over a stone wall just as I was passing. It ran off after staggering around for a while but I doubt if it survived. And the damage to my car came to £3,000! I expected the lady on the phone to the insurance company to be a bit sceptical about this claim but she cheerfully offered that they receive about 45,000 such claims every year. Poor deer. If you're out on a clear autumn or winter morning with blue skies and cold temperatures you may be lucky enough to witness the impact of the overnight temperature inversion which fills the valleys with crisp white cloud whilst the sky above is clear. The journey then alternates between bright blue sky and sparkling white valleys and thick fog. On other days you won't see much at all because it's cloudy and raining.

Well, an hour has passed and you've reached Bellingham - it's on the Pennine Way trail - and you might feel like a break. But no, onwards for another 30 minutes to Kielder village, passing en route the large grassy barrier which is the Kielder Dam (1976) which looms threateningly over the bijou village of Falstone. Nice tea room and pub here but you haven't got time. Another nine miles on with good views of Kielder Water - might see an osprey if you're lucky, it's summer, the weather is clear and you're not driving. Since you passed the dam, you'll have noticed towering conifers on either side of the road and everywhere in the distance. You're in the forest now. Finally, you hope, we reach Kielder village where the main features are the Forestry England depot, Kielder Castle and Dennis's house. You'll meet Dennis later. Kielder Castle is not a castle. It is an ex-hunting lodge built for the Duke of Northumberland in the 19th century. Now it acts as a visitor centre and is adjacent to the start of the Forest Drive, a 12-mile toll road which links the village to the A68. This road closes for the winter months so don't be tempted to try it for a pretty Xmas drive. There are some public toilets in Kielder here too. You might be needing them and there are none beyond this point. And this isn't the end of the journey. After that toilet stop or maybe picking up some equipment from the depot, we're off onto the aforementioned Forest Drive. Don't forget to pay the toll as you enter, unless you're in an NWT vehicle or a bin lorry. Now we follow the Forest Drive for a few miles noticing that the tarmac has given way to a pot-holed gravel track. Then we carry on where the drive goes right and after another mile veer left up a steep bank, sharp right and down the hill past a pond which sometimes turns purple. Keep your eyes open now for feral goats which roam these parts. There are a few hundred of them in the hills around here. Eventually the track runs out, only a mile or so from the Scottish border. We've arrived at the top of the Scaup Burn valley and this is where we find the Wildwood.

Did you enjoy the journey? This is the trip that volunteers have made on many occasions to participate in creating the Kielderhead Wildwood. Crammed into a vehicle with up to nine others with tools, trees, waterproofs, bait* and the emergency welfare bag in the boot. On arrival several hours of demanding work are ahead. And at the end of the day the return journey. Those nine bodies are now either very wet or very sweaty. Conversation soon wanes and snores can be heard from the back seat. Unless Morris is with us and there's another bloody quiz.

* "Bait" is a term used by those from UpNorth to refer to what people in more southern areas would politely refer to as their "packed luncheon". This is not to be confused with the use of such foodstuffs to tempt others into any particular activity which the baiter desires. This confusion was likely when activities were being led by the famous Naomi Waite who would persuade volunteers to join her Magnificent Meadows project by providing homemade cake at the midday break. I like cakes.

"There he got out the luncheon basket and packed a simple meal, in which, remembering the stranger's origins and preferences, he took care to include a yard of long French bread, a sausage out of which the garlic sang, some cheese which lay down and cried, and a long-knocked straw-covered flask wherein lay bottled sunshine shed and garnered on far Southern slopes".
(Kenneth Grahame: *Wind in the Willows*)

N.B. No alcohol was consumed during these adventures despite the fact that the local brewer - The First and Last - produced a beer labelled "Ratty Ale" in support of the project.

I was first persuaded to join in with this form of green gym activity by NWT's Heinz Traut. I was sitting having a relaxing cuppa in the kitchen when Heinz approached. I should have been more wary. "Mel, you know Kielder quite well after playing around with those water voles. How do you fancy a bit of tree planting up there?" It seemed an odd suggestion in a forest of over 100 million trees but I decided to humour him. And I always enjoy the chance to get out into the wilds a bit.

As it turned out Heinz & Co. had come up with a cracking idea in partnership with the Forestry Commission. (Yes, they were called that before they became Forestry England, with their shiny new silver vans.) The aim was to take one of the highest and remotest valleys in the Kielder area and to reintroduce native woodland onto the unforested slopes of the Scaup Burn. At this point I should mention that the word "slope" can imply something gentle, pastoral, imbued with a sense of mindfulness. Not these slopes!

Maya wonders if it would help if one leg was shorter than the other.

More like boulder strewn crags, disguised by bracken to trap the careless tree planter. And that's after having to ford the raging torrent that the Scaup Burn can be, carrying stakes, trees and tools. Oh, for a team of Sherpas! Actually, we had the leadership of Stephen for a while and he did a very good imitation of a Sherpa.

Fording the stream always reminds me of the team of volunteers from Newcastle University who joined us for a gentle day of tree planting a few years ago. A team of about a dozen young men and women turned up in state-of-the-art designer wellies and trainers and took some persuading to accept the offer of more practical waders (ruins the image) to cross the stream. Heinz and the gang had rigged up a rope across the stream, for support when crossing the slippery underwater rocks. I was stationed in the centre of the stream to offer further support and suppress my own giggles (cruel!) when one of them stumbled.

As one of the gang reached the middle of the stream she slipped and fell toward the icy waters, but as she did so her arm shot out - not for help but to grab her phone and take a selfie! With amazing skill she managed to do this whilst regaining her balance and then nonchalantly completed the crossing. Young people are amazing. Laurence is quite good too as can be seen in the photo below.

Yes, sometimes it rains, or pours, or sleets, or hails. And sometimes the sun shines and it's glorious. Why do we always do these tasks in the winter when the weather is at its worst? Whether it's coir dams on top of Whitelee Moor or planting trees on the upper slopes. Well, there is a good reason. These areas are of particular value

Lawrence enjoys the weather and wonders about tomorrow.

to our increasingly threatened ground-nesting birds. Golden plover, curlew, lapwing and more start to nest and lay their eggs in early spring and they're not ready to vacate the premises until autumn. We can't risk disturbing them, and Natural England would intervene if we did. So late autumn and winter it is. Just get those long-johns on and wrap up well. A few characters who think they know better have turned up in denim jeans and a slight waterproof jacket thinking they'll be fine. They weren't. It's really annoying when a task has to abandoned or finished early to prevent them from developing hypothermia. Honestly, some people! They were told.

But over the last few years various and assorted members of the team, now under the more subtle leadership of Natasha and Graham have defied all the odds and planted thousands of native trees in this fabulous and remote valley. Eventually we may see the tree line climb to the top of the valley and cascade over into Scotland. That would be a sight to see.

Other sights to see have included occasional visits by the local population of wild goats which occupy these hills. Being much less easily spooked than the local roe deer, these animals sometimes allow us to get quite close. With the wind in the right direction, they have quite a distinctive aroma. Buzzards and kestrels can also be seen, and if you're lucky an osprey or a goshawk, reptiles too. Maybe even a water vole as one of our release areas was very close by.

There have been a number of key logistical issues involved in the Wildwood scheme:

1. How do you get a team of volunteers from Gosforth to the Scaup Burn in time to have a coffee and plant a few trees before having to set off home again?
2. How to cross the Scaup Burn when it's in a bad mood? The largest areas of planting have been on the opposite side of the burn to the track which gets us up there. Solution A was the aforementioned rope support + wellies or, preferably waders. Many wellies have been filled in the process and at least one member of the team has had an involuntary introduction to "wild swimming". Later on, solution B was to persuade the FC to put in a rough track to the planting area. This at least enabled the transport of the materials to the right place whilst the team still had to brave the crossing of the torrent.
3. How to get the trees and the rest of the gear up the near-vertical, boulder-smattered slopes to the planting area? Use a helicopter! Volunteers still had to make the ascent unaided! Not such a problem in the initial stages when the planting was mainly done on the valley floor and on the lower slopes but it became more of an issue as the planting area expanded. And so, yes, a helicopter was hired to drop the stakes and tree guards on the higher slopes. Often amongst

tall bracken which led to the next fun exercise of clambering around in the bracken trying to find them.

4. How to find a wallet which someone has carelessly dropped whilst stumbling around in the rain planting trees? We searched for ages. Repeatedly retracing our steps during the day and hoping to find a small brown - same colour as bracken at this time of year - leather object nestled amongst the boulders. Needle in a haystack? Simple in comparison. Needless to say, we failed and said volunteer went home in a sulk to cancel his cards and count whatever money he had left. Next time out, as we paused for breath and oxygen on the ascent to tree planters' heaven, a small voice cried out, "Anyone lost a wallet?" Amazing. In this wilderness to stumble across a small object such as this. I suspect a passing feral goat had picked it up, flicked through it and found nothing interesting or edible and left it on a prominent boulder. I do have some strange thoughts.

But it's great to go back now and see young trees emerging amongst the bracken and the boulders. The goats seem to be interested too.

A final highlight for me was assisting with the construction of the drystone wall structure at the viewpoint. Expertly led by two members (Peter and Paul) of the Drystone Wall Society Stephen, Dave Duffy and I completed the task in 2 days. Peter and Paul could probably have done it in one without our help. Our skills had been honed on a day's training session at the RSPB's Geltsdale Reserve. Having a minuscule bit of experience in this craft is very enlightening. A day of dry-stone walling left me with sore fingers, an aching back, tremendous respect for those who do this on a regular basis and a great sense of self-worth.

One of the main reasons for choosing the Scaup Burn for this project was its unique feature of being possibly the only remaining home of the native English Scots pine. Known as the William's Cleugh Pines only a handful remained. It is thought that they had survived because of this very remote location and inhospitable terrain which made commercial use of the land for farming or forestry very marginal. These trees have provided a seed stock from which hundreds more have been grown on and planted out in the valley. Unfortunately, one of the best, and probably oldest of these Scots pine was felled by Storm Arwen in 2022. To us this was particularly sad as that tree was the focal point of the new wildwood and often depicted in pictures portraying what the wood might look like in the future. It is hoped that these pines and the thousands of birch, alder, and willow which have been planted will act as a seed source which will enable the wildwood to expand further along and up the valley to the natural treeline without any further help. Above this will be the highland moors of heather and sphagnum moss and the montane flowers which can thrive there. I've mentioned bog asphodel before but we can also see lesser twayblade, marsh lousewort, butterwort (carnivorous), bilberry and - one of my favourites - cloudberry. Lovely large white flower on that one. And the red berries are edible - but take care, they're also recommended as a laxative.

Chapter 6

Guarding Neville's New Home.

Mink Watch.
OK. Let's get back to those water voles and mink.

As we've heard, a condition of the funding was that we first carried out a monitoring programme to ensure that there was no significant threat from mink in the area selected for the release. Releasing water voles as a ready meal for mink was not part of the plan. The method we used was the deployment of a number of "mink rafts" and trail cameras around the forest. These would be checked for sign of mink on a fortnightly basis.

Any sign of mink would be followed by the setting of humane traps within, or close by the rafts. These traps had to be checked daily, usually by Forestry Commission rangers. Some of the rangers quite enjoyed the variety this gave to their usual job which consisted largely of culling roe deer. Up to 3,000 deer need to be culled each year in order to keep numbers at a sustainable level. This culling is necessary in an area where deer numbers quickly get out of hand because of the lack of apex predators to control their numbers. Maybe lynx should be reintroduced to the area to help with the problem! That's a whole other story.

OK. But what is a mink raft?

John checks it whilst Dave records the result.

Here we can see a raft floating in a large pond. Inside the housing is a basket containing damp clay which will record the print of any animal exploring this new feature of its environment. We've recorded, amongst a few other things, lots of small mammal prints (shrew, field vole etc) + otter, stoat, pine marten and, occasionally, mink.

The original mink raft was developed in 2001 by the Game and Wildlife Conservancy Trust (GWCT), a body set up to protect the interests of the shooting and game fishing industry. Mink don't only eat voles of course. They are a major predator of ground-nesting birds and of fish. So, if you're managing a fishery or a game shoot you won't be fond of mink. Although my attitude toward the game industry is at best ambiguous, it has to be admitted that control of mink on their lands has been of benefit to the water vole. But not of much benefit to many of our raptors, such as the hen harrier and the red kite. The mink raft has the benefit of being pretty low technology, both easy to construct and maintain. Full instructions for making a raft are given in the GWCT's "Guide to American Mink". Too time-consuming for an operation of our magnitude where over 100 such rafts have been deployed and so some of our grant had to be spent on purchasing ready-made kits. The first rafts were made using plywood "sandwiches" with a sheet of polystyrene as the filling to give buoyancy. Later iterations have used plastic sheeting to replace the plywood to increase the longevity of the raft. On top of the flat base is the housing which protects the clay basket enclosed within, and which may attract passing mammals to explore within this intriguing tunnel. Inside the tunnel is a plastic basket which is largely filled with a block of florist oasis which holds water well and keeps the clay layer damp. About two centimetres of a clay/sand mix is added above the oasis. The clay will stay damp for several weeks in favourable conditions and will record the tracks of any animal which walks across it.

Team members always enjoyed starting the day by mixing some clay for the basket – potter's clay + sand + a little water + a lot of kneading = satisfaction. Good to see that Joel had his head down.

The mink raft then needs to be placed in the water, stream or pond, where monitoring for mink is desired. It is important to choose the exact location with care so as to avoid spots where the water flow becomes too turbulent during high water. We have learnt quite a lot about this positioning through trial and error. A couple of errors have led to rafts being badly damaged or in one case entirely lost. After the raft has been in the water for a couple of seasons, especially in Kielder's wild waters, we have seen some worrying deterioration of the polystyrene filling leading to its disintegration and loss. A few clay baskets have also been lost, along with the oasis. To mitigate against any damage to the environment we tried a number of strategies.

- Rafts were replaced when they began to show signs of wear and tear.
- The polystyrene layer was wrapped in a layer of black plastic sheeting to prevent disintegration with access for water to keep the oasis wet.
- In winter, or sites with very rough water we trialled the use of what we christened the "land-based raft" or LBR. At first this simply involved lifting the raft from the water and placing it on level ground alongside a stream. The plastic basket was then replaced with a waterproof tub filled with water to keep the oasis wet and the clay damp. It worked quite well. At one of our sites on the Plashetts Burn we began to see water vole prints regularly whereas the raft when floating in the stream had never had a print over a two-year lifespan. This was one of our first clues that our voles might not always be sticking to the conventional rules about travelling along the waterways. They themselves seemed to be more land-based. Our very first attempt at this used disused ice cream tubs of a suitable size. So, you may come across the term ice cream raft (ICR) on some of my weekly reports. Unfortunately, this practice involved someone having to empty the ice cream tub of its

original contents first. Raspberry ripple, caramel or just plain vanilla (my personal favourite). Volunteers were usually quite willing to do this. More willing than they usually were to spend an hour making up some more clay for the baskets!

- We were also a bit concerned about the use of the oasis as this is also a product of the petrochemical industry. Whilst very few of these have been lost, we thought we might try alternatives. With the help of volunteer Dr. Wendy we came up with a couple of trials. First, we tried sphagnum moss, of which there is a plentiful supply in Kielder Forest. This worked quite well on the LBRs (you will remember that's a land-based raft - keep paying attention). But there was a tendency for the moss to dry out too quickly and when the clay needed replacing, we found the moss and clay had combined in a mushy layer and so the whole filling had to be replaced. Good try but not as easy or reliable as the oasis. Next we tried coir. Again, worked OK, but with the same problem when it came to changing the clay.

Enough of that. What to do if mink tracks were found on inspection of the clay?

That's the time for urgent action. Mink can cover considerable distances and may come and go in an area. Unless it's a breeding female which has decided to make this her territory. In which case it's even more urgent to catch her before breeding begins. So, as soon as tracks are reported a humane trap is placed inside the housing of the mink raft. This is baited with something suitably smelly to attract the mink. Some use fish paste or cat food which both seem to work. As we've read, some use the attractive smelling extract from the mink's anal scent gland. Well, it is attractive if you're another mink. These traps must then be checked twice a day to prevent undue distress to any animal caught. Anything apart from a mink would be released immediately. A mink must be dispatched as quickly and humanely as possible. It is illegal to release a mink once trapped. And please apologise to the mink and forgive yourself if you have done this out of necessity and without taking any pleasure in it. If you have done this for fun, please see a counsellor as soon as possible.

Ken and Sue seem to have found something interesting.

Monitoring Teams & Routes

But how were we going to manage the monitoring of all of these rafts, and later trail cameras which were added to give us another perspective on what was going on in the forest. Our range didn't cover the whole 250 square miles of the entire forest, but it covered a pretty big percentage of it. A maze of forest trails had to be navigated and the FC had thoughtlessly neglected to install any sort of signposting system. No traffic lights or roundabouts either. And with a round trip from NWT headquarters in Gosforth, Newcastle adding up to 160 miles plus, with up to 50 miles of this being on forest tracks, a team of drivers would be needed.

The original plan was to divide the area we needed to monitor into four segments. Each segment would have its own lead volunteer who would have the responsibility to monitor their patch accompanied by at least one other volunteer. These lead volunteers either had previous training from NWT or were to receive it before they began. This training included health & safety, risk assessment, first aid, safe use of tools and familiarisation with trust vehicles. The original four leads being myself, Don Learmouth, Steve Harris and John Bower. Steve was immediately overflowing with his customary enthusiasm and before we knew it, he had produced detailed maps from OS extracts showing the location of each of our original raft locations. These were extremely useful as we struggled to get to know our routes. Tom Dearnley, FC Ecologist who was leading on the FC part of the project, and chairing the partnership Restoring Ratty board, and some of his rangers, took some time out to give us an initial tour of the routes. It took a few days out on our own to fully get to grips with the geography of the forest. Several wrong turns and blind alleys later, we were getting to know our way around quite well. And this familiarisation has had to be repeated most years as those lead volunteers moved on and have been replaced by others, notably Sue Cornick, Dave Duffy, Simon Parker and most recently John Wollaston and Ellesse Janda. It is impossible to imagine how the project could have proceeded as effectively as it did without these leaders. All with their own unique and varied skills and approaches to the tasks required. And in addition to them a host of other volunteers and staff have contributed to the monitoring, surveying and, most excitingly, the releases. Most of these via their membership of NWT but also significant numbers from the Tyne Rivers Trust. Special thanks must go to Forestry Commission staff Paul, Dan, Wayne and more. Without their help, particularly with the early releases, we would have struggled.

It soon became obvious because of staffing and vehicle pressures that the four area system was having problems with consistently checking the rafts as often as was needed. So we shifted to a bipartite regime of having two more or less circular routes each of which could be managed in a day. Each route would be checked once a fortnight. The two current routes are shown on the diagram below. Whilst these have changed almost annually to reflect the new release sites the general pattern has been retained. Kielder Water has proven to be a useful focal point for devising the routes, although it is not often visible from the depths of the forest. You can soon get lost as the dense canopy of the Sitka spruce closes in around you. Which reminds me of some useful information which was passed on to us by Rachel, one of our frequent volunteers. Rachel is a very keen conservation volunteer and has dwarfed our efforts by participating in volunteer projects in areas as diverse as Outer Mongolia (raptors), the Galapagos Islands (invasives) and Iceland (forestry). When in Iceland she was given the following advice when asking what to do if you were to get lost in the Icelandic forest: "Stand up" was the reply.

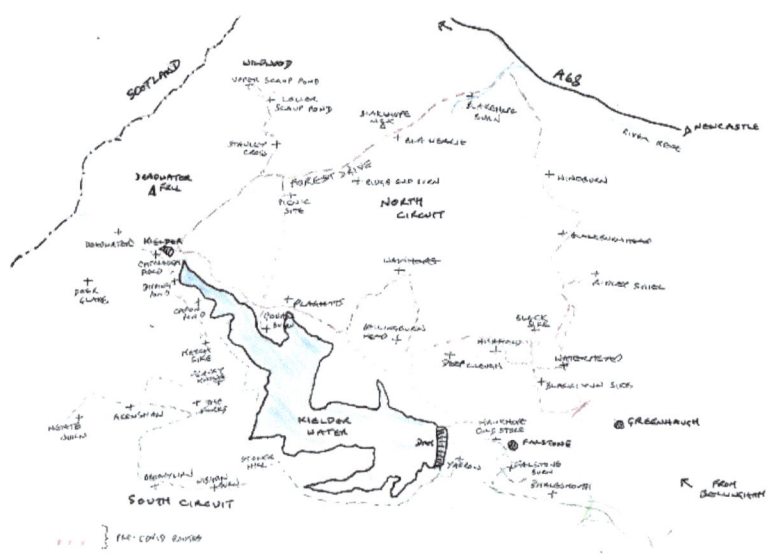

Mink Raft Monitoring

Trees don't grow so well there. Not much use in Kielder, I'm afraid. You wouldn't want to try forcing yourself through or up these conifers which can be quite painful on the skin.

As you will see the routes can be separated by the reservoir into a higher route to the north and east of the reservoir and a slightly lower but still quite hilly south and west route. The higher route is almost entirely off road, following the North Haul Road along the edge of the reservoir before emerging in Kielder village and joining the Forest Drive to traverse the watershed between the North Tyne and the River Rede. After descending from the highest point on the Forest Drive at Blakehope Nick, the route then follows the Pennine Way for a few miles and finally emerging from the forest close to the small village of Greenhaugh and the tiny Holly Inn where the locals have fond memories of Derek Gow's visit in 2017. Most of them have since recovered.

John bags a Christmas Tree for free. Or was he helping Dave to clear the way? I was sitting comfortably in the cab.

The more southerly route uses the public road from the Kielder dam to Kielder Village and beyond as its spine with various diversions into the forest proper and passing close to the Kielder Observatory and the delightfully named Deadwater Fell.

As mentioned earlier these routes have changed over the years to take account of new vole release areas. In preparation for each year's releases we would make sure that there were mink rafts located close to these sites for several months in advance. Occasionally we would move rafts which didn't seem to be serving any real purpose or where we were having problems with maintaining them because of streams which were just too violent. For instance our raft on the rather romantically named "Oh Me Sike"* on the northern route. We were regularly losing the clay from the basket and then one day it just wasn't there any more! There had been heavy rain and most of the streams were high but this one was obviously in a very violent stage. It's only a very small, innocent-looking but rather steep little stream in a beautiful setting high up on the Forest Drive. But the raft had completely disappeared. A search downstream was conducted. Difficult because of the steep and rocky ground, including by-passing a couple of small waterfalls. But no sign of the raft, not even a bit of wreckage. Perhaps it will turn up one day. Maybe several miles downstream in Kielder Water. This is the only raft we've completely lost. Others have broken free and been found a few hundred yards downstream. One was found up a tree! That flood must have been extremely high. Either that or the raft had developed aero-dynamic qualities and flown up there. It was interesting work getting it down anyway.

* *There are some interesting names around this part of Northumberland. Some seem quite obscure but worth recalling. A local amateur historian made it his task to mark some of these with stone slabs, rather like memorial stones. On these he has carefully chiselled out the relevant names and then carried each one, weighing several kilos each - or a couple of stone in old speak -,*

to the correct spot and then dug them in. What a task. "Oh Me Sike" is one of them which we have come across. That is the name of this little stream. You can check it on the OS map for Kielder Forest if you don't believe me. Other interesting names marked in this way and on our routes include "Bla Wearie", Bubbling Spring" and "Stanley Cross". We don't know why Stanley was cross but there are at least two Bla Wearies in the county. Apparently, the term can be translated as a "lazy wind" which, as folks in Edinburgh will confirm, is applied to a cold easterly wind which is too lazy to blow around you, so it blows straight through you. Or at least it feels as though it does. And the Bubbling Spring is a particularly interesting one. There is a pond alongside the Scaup Burn - that's where the Kielderhead Wildwood is to be found - fed by this underground spring which can be seen bubbling up in the corner of the pond. As it is fed from below ground this water is relatively warm and doesn't get cold in the winter. And so this pond rarely freezes over and seems to be very popular with the local newt population. We have found up to 15 of these nestled together within the raft in the early spring. This pond is also subject to a strange phenomenon which we first noticed in 2018. As we arrived to check the raft, parking a few metres above it, we could see some strange purple-coloured patches in the water. The first ones we saw were quite close to the bubbling spring. Strange. Next time out the patches had grown and more had appeared. After a few weeks the whole pond was coloured purple. Had there been purple rain? (Apologies to those formerly known as Prince fans). We were rather concerned about this phenomenon as it appeared to be killing off some of the vegetation in the pond and we had released a number of voles close by. Water samples were taken and sent off for analysis. The phenomenon turned out to be caused by purple sulphur bacteria. I'm no scientist but as far as I understand it this group of bacteria feed via photosynthesis but without the need for oxygen. At particular temperatures the bacterium appears under water and feeds on organic *compounds, in this case the decaying vegetation in the pond. Blooms of this bacterium can become dominant in the pond and cause eutrophication, denying oxygen to life in the pond by blocking out the light. Interestingly any signs of water voles have disappeared since the pond first turned purple. Since that first sighting the pond gradually returned to normal, although less dominant occurrences have been seen since, and at the time of writing there seems to be another major growth on the way.*

Whilst these days of monitoring the area for mink were primarily about establishing a safe haven for the voles, we soon developed a wider interest. At first a successful day would be counted as one where we found no sign of mink, and the vehicle we were travelling in survived without mishap. At the end of each day one of the team leaders would write a brief report for the management team. The condition of each raft was recorded together with any sign of mink. This was a rarity but when it did happen traps would be set in the relevant raft and in the immediate surroundings. Initially the trapping - and the dispatch of any mink which were unwise enough to be in the area - was carried out by Forestry England staff. Later, with the inception of the Naturally Native project, this would fall to their local member of staff, the indomitable and unforgettable Emily Marshall. In the ten years of the project only a handful of mink were caught. The areas where they were caught indicated that they were mink which were entering the target zone from one of two directions. Either over the border from Scotland and appearing in the proximity of Kielder Village or moving up the valley of the North Tyne and arriving in the approaches to the Kielder dam. We became fairly confident that the forest itself did not contain a resident mink population.

All this was very good, but it did mean that our attention began to need some other stimulation during these long days. And our reports became somewhat embellished by records of non-mink findings on the rafts or sightings of various examples of the local flora and fauna. Sometimes unusual events or places took our attention too. A couple of examples of these reports can be seen in the appendix. Sadly, in some ways, although management may disagree, these reports became redundant with the development of technology to record our days out. A few clicks on the app and we were done. But this tended to obscure the unique experiences of the day. See what you think. It might not be science.

As the seasons progressed, the focus of our days changed too. In winter our main concerns would centre on the weather and the impact this had on the rafts, and ourselves as we trudged around. In very cold weather the clay in the baskets would freeze so that no tracks could be discerned. In very wet weather the streams would rage and rafts could be damaged. We soon learned that in these waters it was best to secure the clay basket to the raft with wire to prevent it from being washed away. And in high winds there was the danger that fallen trees would block our way. After severe weather forestry staff would warn us to stay away if they judged it to be unsafe and we would postpone the checks. In this way mishaps were avoided but we did have a couple of close shaves. Ellesse will remember one icy day when emerging from the forest onto the public road, she touched the brakes only to find the van sliding gracefully across the main road. Thankfully with no traffic around. And once when Simon was in the driving seat, we had experienced both ice and wind. As we approached Deep Cleugh we could see a fallen tree ahead. A medium sized Sitka too big to move and completely blocking the road. OK, we knew of an alternative forest track and set off to find the other way. Only to find that route blocked by a large fallen pine tree. What now? Give up and retrace our steps? The more nervous members of the crew began to wonder what would happen if a tree had fallen across the track upon which we had earlier entered the forest. Would we be stuck here for days? What would we eat? The rest of the crew didn't look very appetising. (No offence guys.) Luckily scrutiny of the OS map - they are useful - revealed a final alternative and we made it out of forest at the dam and unscathed. Time to give up and go home? No, we took a deep breath and carried on around the rest of the route with no mishaps. And there was once with only Sue, Don and me in the van when we began to wonder if the snow was just a bit too deep as we approached the highest point on the Forest Drive. All other vehicle tracks had long since ceased. It was hard to accept with only one raft left to check, obviously frozen over anyway, but we decided on discretion above valour, and gingerly set off back down the snowy track to the relative civilisation of Kielder village.

Early on in the project vehicles were a bit of an issue too. An initial thought had been that volunteers might be happy to use their own vehicles. Our preliminary trip around the forest and a perusal of insurance policies led to this idea being abandoned. Instead, we were given access to one of NWT's vehicles, usually a small Peugeot van which Don loved to drive around the forest. Don is an ex-police driver and rarely daunted by any problems on these rough tracks. In spite of our suggestions that a more robust vehicle, preferably four-wheel drive, might be more appropriate, the powers that be decided that seeing as we were mainly driving on forestry tracks, we should be OK. Have you seen some of these tracks? Some of them are barely distinguishable from the surrounding vegetation. Anyway, this came to a head when Don and I were driving merrily along one summer's day and I had to advise Don that it might be wise to pull over as the rear up-and-over door was now lying on the track some way behind us. The bolts holding the door in place had sheared off, probably because of the constant vibrations over the previous few months. Subsequently we were usually allowed access to the four-wheel drive and high clearance of the L200. It came to little harm but it did let us down once in the forest when it simply refused to start. No phone signal, remember. We did always carry an SOS device which could alert emergency services to any disaster but this wasn't that severe a problem. So, off we trekked on foot to find the nearest land line. Luckily only a mile or so away at this point. It could have been a lot worse. Latterly we have had the use of our trusty Isuzu which has put up with many miles of rough ground, clawed its way out of muddy terrain and rarely let us down. Just a few punctures which you can't blame on the vehicle. But it's not much fun lying on a muddy track trying to wind down the spare wheel, finding a reasonably level spot for the jack in the pouring rain as the sun goes down. All good fun. Only one careful owner - several less trustworthy drivers? We won't talk about the various dents and missing bits of bodywork.

"Glorious, stirring sight!" murmured Toad…..”The poetry of motion! The real way to travel! The only way to travel! here today - in next week tomorrow! Villages skipped, towns and cities jumped - always somebody else's horizons! O bliss! O poop-poop! O my! O my!"

(Kenneth Grahame: *Wind in the Willows***)**

Sue has perfected her "Scandinavian flick" on the gravel tracks since we were met by a car rally in full swing on one of our rounds.

As members of the Northumberland Wildlife Trust, we were obviously very interested in the flora and fauna in the forest. John could often be found in a stream turning over the stones to find caddis fly larvae or other fascinating invertebrates whilst Sue had her binoculars trained on the horizon as she sought out the local raptors. Once he emerged from the stream, John would then be on the hunt for as many types of bee as he could identify. On occasions I would be on my knees inspecting some wildflower that we had come across. In our last year we decided to list as many wildflowers as we could identify in the forest. Unfortunately, our work came to an end before a full year was complete. Nevertheless, a list of the flowers we did identify is attached at the end of the book. During the spring and summer months our reports often included "Flower of the Day" and very briefly "Duck of the Day" which sometimes turned out to be a goose.

In addition to the infrequent spotting of a water vole - big cheers - we also spotted roe deer on 95% of our trips. These are the only native deer found in the forest, although there have been the odd unconfirmed reports of muntjac. And the roe deer numbers are high and a concern for both Forestry England and NWT on its neighbouring Whitelee Nature Reserve. When uncontrolled by any natural predator the deer multiply rapidly and can cause great damage to young trees, hedgerows and some of the more vulnerable plants. In a commercial forest or a wildlife reserve it can be necessary to control the numbers. From a nature perspective the benefits of reducing deer numbers can be seen to great effect in the Carrifran Wildwood over the border in the Scottish Southern Uplands. Here a landscape previously bereft of native wildflowers, insects and songbirds has been transformed by the planting of over 300,000 trees and the control of grazing by deer and sheep. The valley floor is now a riot of colour and birdsong in the summer, with flowers unseen for decades appearing along the stream side. One interesting example being the possibly misnamed sea campion. Before rewilding of the valley, this beautiful little flower, commonly seen on sea cliffs, was only found on high and inaccessible crags at the head of the valley. Once the sheep had been removed and the deer managed effectively, the flower began to appear lower and lower down the slopes until now it is abundant on the valley floor. And this happened with no replanting efforts. Seeds from the high crags were washed down the slope and quickly took root in the much more congenial land below. Any attempts to spread prior to this had been thwarted by the grazing animals, especially the sheep who like tender young growth.

In Kielder Forest the roe deer are recognised as native animals and there is no desire to rid the area of these very attractive inhabitants. But their impact on tree growth is too severe in a commercial forest or a wildwood if numbers are not controlled. As a result, Forestry England employ a group of rangers whose main duty is to stalk and shoot a sufficient number of deer to keep the population stable. Currently they are removing around 3,000 deer each year. The deer are then sold on to local butchers for sale as venison or into the pet food chain. One day I asked Dan, one of the rangers, how many deer there are in the forest. His reply was that they don't have an accurate estimate of numbers but that they know that the removal of these 3,000 keeps the population stable and manageable.

The other large mammal which we come across quite regularly is the feral goat. Descended from domestic stock in the sixteenth century there are now several hundred of these goats roaming the higher fells around Kielder and the Cheviot area. They are attractive to see, not always so nice to smell if you get too close at the wrong time of year. Unfortunately, these goats are even worse than the roe deer for damaging young trees and hedges, and regular attempts are made to move them from one area of the fell to another. Again, the numbers need to be controlled which does mean an occasional cull. However, numbers involved are much smaller than for the deer. On our travels, sightings of roe deer tend to be fleeting as the animals are highly nervous - they've probably heard about those rangers - and quickly disappear into the woodland from which they rarely stray. The goats on the other hand are far less timid and will usually stop and have a good stare at us before slowly ambling off. It may be that the introduction of a few Eurasian lynx, once native in these hills, would help to control and manage the movement of these deer and goats. There is a long-standing proposal to do this but it is a far more contentious issue than reintroducing some cuddly voles or even a few beavers. Local farmers are understandably concerned about the threat to their sheep and lambs, even young calves. Dog walkers and parents have also expressed concern about the presence of this quite large predator. Whilst it is claimed that the lynx would prey entirely on the roe deer, hares and rabbits, those responsible for the proposal have not done a very good job of persuading the local population that this is the case. We wait to see whether this might happen in the near future. I think wolves and brown bear are still some way off. But I do suspect that the first controlled beaver release in the forest may not be too far away. We have already seen a popular and so-far successful reintroduction of these great landscape architects on the National Trust's Wallington Estate not too far away.

Don was driving so this group of goats decided to get a move on

What is the link between feral goats and wildflowers? I like them both but that's not the answer. One day last summer I decided to go for a walk up onto Whitelee Moor, right on the Scottish border. My aim was to see the bog asphodel in flower. Rumour had it that it was blooming prolifically on top of the moor. So I set off quite early from the car park at Carter Bar on the Scottish border and waved farewell to the piper who regularly haunts this lay-by as he waits to assault coach loads of Italian and Japanese tourists with his desirable wares: CDs capturing his wonderful Scottish ballads and authentic handmade dolls with kilts celebrating the various clans. Thankfully I was soon out of earshot and struggling along the boggy path. After an hour or so I passed the cairn at the top of

Carter Pike and then paused to watch the birds over Buzzard Crag. Yes, they were buzzards. Further on I finally reached the old lime kilns and the ruins of the workers cottages. Wild flowers abounded here. Marsh lousewort, tormentil, clovers and heather. But not much bog asphodel yet. So, a quick cup of coffee and onwards toward the border. Another 20 minutes and I finally reached the top. Here the slope evened out and before me lay acres of the flower I was after. The individual flower is a very attractive yellow to orange bloom but in the thousands spread out before me it was truly spectacular. Well worth the effort to get there. And as I gazed around and took a few photos I noticed some movement on the skyline. Another strange flower seeker perhaps. No, it was a large billy goat and with him a small family of females and kids. At first, they kept wandering toward me, oblivious to my presence I suspect. But then he stopped and stared directly toward me, trying to make out what he was seeing, I guess. His nose sniffed the air. A rather arrogant pose I thought. I suspect he had caught the scent of my houmous sandwiches, rather garlicky. Whatever it was, he slowly turned his back, beckoned to the family and slowly wandered off toward Scotland. I watched them for several minutes until they eventually dropped from view. Never hurrying, no panic. Their domain, not mine. What a privilege and a delight. Masses of flowers and a communion of sorts with this impressive animal. Are they invasive? Or just Scottish? Great to see anyway. Then, after the rush of blood and a while soaking in the surrounding beauty on a glorious day it was time to head on back to the bagpipes. Fortunately, by the time I got back to the car he'd packed up and gone. There is such a thing as bagpipe fatigue, I think. But it sounds hauntingly attractive from a distance. When I finally reached the car, levering off those boots from my weary feet, I realised that I had been away for 6 hours and in all that time I hadn't seen a single human. It had been bliss.

What about Sue's raptors? They aren't the only birds we've seen in the forest. Herons are regularly seen and common in the area, as

Neville could testify if he were still with us. The jay is also often seen along with smaller songbirds such as chaffinch and occasionally crossbills. And we have often sat on the banks of the Scaup Burn eating our bait (lunch) as the sand martins hunted over the stream and over our heads. But the raptors steal the show. Top of the tree, excuse the pun, must be the extremely rare but once spotted golden eagle. So far there are none of these birds currently resident in the forest but a small population exists across the border in the upper reaches of the Tweed catchment. An attempt to increase the numbers was made a few years ago by the release of a few birds taken from the Highlands on the nature reserve at Langholm. Not far at all from Kielder as the eagle flies. And in 2022 a bird was spotted by a highly reliable source on the high moors at the head of the Scaup Burn valley. Just above our Wildwood plantation. The same, most likely, or a similar bird was seen a couple of times more by the rangers and once by our very own spotter, Sue. Lucky Sue. It would be wonderful to see these magnificent birds once again flying over Northumberland and, who knows it may not be too long.

We have already heard about the great success of the osprey project and these are seen by the team quite often in the breeding season. Usually just the one bird, in the action of diving for fish if we're really lucky. But at the end of the season when the young birds are starting to fly and to practise their fishing technique we have seen as many as 4 birds together in the air. One day we had the pleasure and amusement of watching a buzzard attempt to drive an osprey off its perceived territory. The buzzard's only real hope was to get above the osprey and to dive bomb it. Unfortunately for the buzzard this involved a long and drawn-out effort using the thermals to gain enough height before it could attack. Only to be met with disdain by the intended victim which simply flicked its talons at the aggressor and carried serenely along. After several forays the buzzard retired to its perch, probably thinking it had succeeded whereas the truth was the osprey was just passing through anyway. The trouble is raptors just don't like members of other raptor tribes. Ring any bells about some people? You name them, I'm not. Talking of buzzards our record total for one trip stands at 17. Probably now never to be beaten. Probably wouldn't get in the record books as it is a bit niche.

Another star raptor - I know, I thought this book was about voles too - is the hen harrier, which we have seen but far less often than the ospreys and the buzzards. A much-persecuted bird of prey which, unfortunately for its own safety likes to do its hunting over the uplands. The problem here being the grouse shooting lobby. Doesn't meet my criteria for "sport" I'm afraid. But they believe that the hen harrier is a threat to their grouse and, therefore their "pleasure", if you're a sportsman, or their livelihood, if you're a gamekeeper or a beater. Nevertheless, this fabulous bird seems to be making something of a recovery in the last few years. Far too early to celebrate but at least a chink of hope that the persecutors are either growing up or beginning to fear that they might be caught and punished. My personal favourite encounter was with a male bird. They are smaller than the female and have a grey plumage which makes them seem quite ghostly on a misty day. And they fly silently just to enhance the image. This bird was sitting atop a post alongside the Forest Drive as we approached the highest point at Blakehope Nick, just over 1500 ft. As the van passed the bird dropped off the post and drifted alongside us for about 50 yards, just a few feet away and glancing sideways into the van at intervals. probably wondering what on earth we were doing up here. Then he flicked to one side and floated off down the slope. What an experience. Good for the soul. It still gives me goosebumps when I remember those piercing eyes looking into mine. Cath, my wife, has been known to give me that stare - a look of puzzled amusement or awe - I'm not sure which.

Other raptors on our list include the goshawk, the sparrowhawk and the merlin.

Not a bad list. A pity the red kite hasn't made it yet. But it's on the way despite the criminals who have shot and poisoned numbers of birds that have attempted to spread out from their stronghold where they were released in the Derwent Valley.

Male hen harrier

Chapter 7

Where Neville Came From.

"Take the adventure, heed the call, now ere the irrevocable moment passes! 'Tis but a banging of the door behind you, a blithesome step forward, and you are out of your old life and into the new!" ……. the vole thought as he stepped into Roisin's trap.
(Kenneth Grahame: Wind in the Willows)

The Real Work Begins: Phase 2. Finding Some Volunteer Voles for Release

After two years of intensive monitoring, no threat from American mink had been found. As a result, the partnership placed a further bid with the National Lottery Heritage Fund and secured five years funding to reintroduce water voles to Kielder Forest. And so, the Restoring Ratty project was born. Big thanks to the players of the National Lottery!

So much for pleasant days wandering around Kielder Forest in all weathers, watching wildlife and drinking tea. Now the real stuff starts. What are we going to do? We now had permission to release real-life water voles in Kielder Forest. But where were these new voles coming from? Where would we put them? How would we do it? Our new boss would have to lead us, but who was that new boss?

Kelly practises her speaking and listening skills in preparation for the interview.

To help them decide, the partnership board asked Don and me to sit in on the interviews. I think they even listened to our views. As it turned out, there was a lot of interest in the post and some excellent candidates. To make it more difficult most of them performed really well on interview and could provide excellent CVs. In the end it was agreed by all parties that the optimum outcome was to appoint the two best candidates to take on a job share. Perfect outcome. Now we had Kelly and Graham. Yes, the same Kelly that we had been working with so far joined by Graham Holyoak who had been working on the project with the Tyne Rivers Trust and would now share his time between them and NWT. They proved to be a great team with complementary skills and a shared sense of humour. They would need it.

Soon we learnt that our next job would be helping to collect some wild water voles to establish a breeding population ready for release. Dr Roisin Campbell-Palmer and her colleague Ben from the Scottish Beaver re-introduction project had been contracted by the Derek Gow Consultancy to assist us by surveying areas of Northumberland where a healthy population of water voles might still exist. This research was carried out meticulously and Roisin's report concluded that there were reasonably healthy water vole populations in the valley of the West Allen River to the south of Allendale town and in the Upper Tees valley around the village of Langdon Beck. It would also be possible to gather some voles from the Trossachs and from the North Yorkshire Moors. Roisin and her team set out to collect up to 40 voles of the right size and gender for the breeding programme in Devon. Quite a task. The licence to collect these voles included a number of stipulations. Numbers taken must not put the donor population under stress and the selected voles must be under 160 grammes in weight, with the collecting being done in the autumn. Why, you might ask. Well, we've already established that winter is a tough time for voles. Food is in short supply; the weather can be severe and hungry predators are in need of protein. Research suggests that any vole weighing less than 160 grammes at the beginning of winter is unlikely to survive. Whereas down in Devon, Derek and his team would put them up in luxury accommodation and feed them well in preparation for their breeding duties in the spring. If you ask me any sensible vole would be likely to make the right choice and join up. And this fits with the fact that these are adolescents in vole life terms. They are likely to have been born in the last or penultimate litter of the year and have not yet had time to reach a size which would give them a reasonable chance of surviving the winter. And like most adolescents many of them will be keen to leave home and escape from those pesky siblings.

For our part in this task, we set out to assist Roisin's team in collecting some wild voles from the upper Allendale area. We collected a few which were transported down to Devon together with some northern compatriots from the Trossachs and the North

Yorkshire Moors. Our voles needed to be northern as there is a genetic difference between the hardier northern vole and the southern cream-tea devouring cousin in the south. But how would we do this collecting?

You will note that I have chosen to use the term "collecting" rather than "trapping", which would probably be more honest. Well, during one of our "collecting" days I was approached by a member of the public, who turned out to be a landowner who lived close by. She asked what we were up to. And when I told her that we were trapping some water voles to take part in the captive breeding programme she became very agitated. Why were we taking her beautiful voles, would there be any left, would they be harmed in the process? All very reasonable questions, I think. Trapping can sound a bit aggressive I suppose. After I had explained the project to her, she calmed down a lot and was happy for us to continue. I decided in future to tell folk that we were collecting volunteer voles for an all-in holiday project in picturesque Devon. It seemed to work.

Roisin with her colleague Ben and members of the Restoring Ratty team. (Kelly, Mel - with the hat on - and Don).

The "collection" process was quite straightforward and unlikely to cause the voles too much stress providing that the rules were followed carefully. The humane trap can be seen in the photograph above. The trap is secured to a small floating raft and placed in the stream close to where surveys had shown signs of water voles. The raft is secured to the side of the bank and baited with some pieces of apple and carrot. Voles like these. A number of rafts are located along a stretch of water and checked at least twice in the day. First thing in the morning and before dark in the evening. This can only be done during reasonable weather otherwise rafts may be washed or blown away or damaged and any captive animal put in danger. If a passing vole is tempted by the smell of the bait, part of its five a day, it might haul up onto the raft and have a chew. Then it notices some more of these tasty morsels inside the metal cage and wanders in, stepping on the sprung plate which releases a catch and lowers the door. After finishing its snack, the vole now realises it can't get back out but that there is a cosy nest of straw in the covered part of the cage. Here they are protected from the elements and settle down for a snooze. Sometime later a kindly human appears and asks them if they would like to take up the offer of a free holiday. The volunteer vole then has to be passed fit by being checked for weight and health. If it passes it is transferred into comfortable single accommodation for the trip south, just like Neville's dad. If it unfortunately fails the test because of its weight it is returned to the point of collection and returned to take its chances back at home where it can try to explain where it's been.

The rafts are only left out for a couple of days and once a few voles have been recruited they are collected in and the local population - vole and human - are left in peace. On my first morning returning to check the rafts I was becoming a little disheartened having inspected about 10 rafts without reward when I moved on to Sparty Lea, close to Dirt Pot for those who don't know the area. However, as I approached Raft 11 - they have to be numbered so that you know where to return any overweight voles which fail the weigh in - I noticed some movement in the bedding area and was delighted to see a very dark, almost black vole emerge from his slumber. So, after reading him the required invitation I detached the cage from the raft, placed it in the boot of my car and drove off to meet Roisin at the designated spot in Allenheads. Roisin carried out the usual checks and confirmed that it was a male. The weight test was passed and he was accepted onto the project. Thinking back, he did look rather like Neville. I wonder if it was Neville's dad.

Roisin and her colleagues repeated this process for several days in Allendale, and nine new voles were added to the collection. Together with a similar number of voles each from the North York Moors and from the Trossachs these made up the new breeding population and were transported down to Devon. Taking voles from a number of different sites in UpNorth was important to ensure that a good mix of genes was added to the population. Also important that all 3 sites were in the north as we have already learned that northern voles are slightly different from their southern cousins. As we now know both populations moved into the area we know as Great Britain after the latest ice age ended about 10,000 years ago. The southern voles originating from what is now France and the northern contingent from north Germany and the Baltic area. Today the two populations tend to be separated by a line roughly drawn between the estuaries of the Humber and the Mersey, although I am sure there is some mixing of populations around this zone. There are probably bilingual voles in this area living around Scunthorpe and Swinefleet.

To help you visualise this whole process you can see three short videos on YouTube if you search for "Restoring Ratty". These focus on 1. The Capture ("Collection"), 2. Breeding in Devon, and 3. The Release.

Down on the Farm.

These "volunteer" voles, probably including Neville's dad, were transported down to one of the few licensed vole breeders in England at Derek Gow's vole stud in Devon. To help us understand what we were in for, a trip to Derek's stud was organised in January 2017. It was great. Derek was a revelation. A tremendously knowledgeable and vocal advocate for the re-introduction of threatened species. Not just water voles but also beavers, cranes, otters, pine marten, wild cats etc. The advice and assistance provided by Derek and his team was invaluable and validating for what we aimed to achieve. It also rained a lot whilst we were there. Good preparation for what we had let ourselves in for.

Derek demonstrates the release pens which we would be using. On subsequent visits to Northumberland, he demonstrated lots of other things.

Derek's breeding centre is based on his farm on the edge of Dartmoor close to the rustically named village of Broadwoodwidger. You couldn't make up that name. Derek previously made his living as a livestock farmer but his great interest and knowledge in wildlife conservation has led to a shift in focus. Nowadays all of his time is spent on breeding, conservation and re-introduction projects.

If you're familiar with the south west of England in January, and particularly with the western edge of Dartmoor, you won't be surprised to learn that when we arrived it was raining, quite hard. So we were pleased that the first part of our visit consisted of an indoor talk and demonstration by Derek. We learnt about "hard" and "soft" releases.

Hard when the voles are taken to a previously scouted site which is deemed to be suitable and released straight into the wild. This has been a technique often used in mitigation projects where voles have been moved when their habitats are disrupted by developments such as new roads or housing estates. This usually involves relatively few animals. We were to concentrate more on the soft release method whereby the voles are placed in secure release pens in their new home area. They are then given a couple of days to acclimatise to the new environment before being given the chance to exit the pen via a baffle board. These are not meant to confuse the voles but to help them decide when to leave.

Derek also gave us a brief but informative talk about how the voles are cared for, with an expert team on hand and the services of the local vet. His centre has more than 100 breeding pens on site and is able to house and care for 1000 voles over the winter. After a thorough health check, voles are then selected for release into the wild in the spring. Well over 2000 voles have been delivered to our "Restoring Ratty" project. In addition to our voles, Derek's team have reared and delivered thousands of others to sites all over the UK.

We tried to keep Derek talking - not all that difficult if you know Derek - with lots of questions but soon we had to get back outside for a tour of the facilities. You guessed it, it was raining. Just a bit harder. But the tour was well worth it. Not just around the water vole breeding pens but the beaver compound too. They quite like all this water. And others; wild cats, polecats, pine marten and cranes included. And then, big thanks to the DG Consultancy team and off we set for home. It was nice and dry in the van but lots of chatter following the visit and all those wet clothes made it rather humid.

Up the Trossachs and Other Release Projects
Then, in May 2017 we were off up to the Trossachs to learn from the Forestry Commission team up there about how they had gone about their successful water vole re-introduction. Faced with a much larger mink problem than we seemed to have, they had a lot of good advice to give us.

The Trossachs project, based in the Forest of Ard close to Aberfoyle, was initially a large-scale mitigation project to rehouse water voles displaced by large-scale development on the outskirts of Glasgow in 2006. Where were they to go? Happily, an opportunity presented itself along the valley of the Duchray river near Aberfoyle. Forestry practice was changing as national priorities changed. To encourage wildlife regeneration, tree cover had been removed from stream sides to provide a corridor for natural vegetation to regrow. Also, streams were re-meandered and pools and lakes created. Associated flora and fauna could then take advantage of this, and bio-diversity could increase. Great place to reintroduce water voles then. But first the local population of mink had to be brought under control. The first water voles, bred from those Glaswegians, were released in 2008. There were 350 of them. Further releases in 2009 and 2010 brought the total to 1000 voles. The project has been a great success with voles having spread well beyond the release area.

The mink have been largely eradicated from the release area. In the early years they were trapping and despatching tens of mink in a year, but by 2017 were down to just the occasional intruder. Care was being taken to guard the periphery of the release area, which becomes increasingly problematic as the water voles spread beyond the boundary, and the remit, of the Forestry Commission. Working with neighbouring landowners brings different issues into the equation and this may well be the case in Northumberland. Whilst most of the landowners in this part of Scotland were sympathetic to the idea of controlling mink on their land it would only take one significant refusenik and the mink would have a safe haven from which to launch forays into the release area and to prevent the spread of water voles into their territory. The FC lead officer for the project - Katy Anderson - made a very telling comment. When asked by her organisation to describe the "exit strategy" for the project, she could only reply, "There is no exit strategy". For as long as the mink remain a threat, vigilance will be needed. And then there are other predators and human action to be monitored. Is there no way out or was she looking for a job for life?

Graham and Don prepare to examine some burrows in the Trossachs

Of course, the Trossachs and Kielder releases are not the only water vole re-introduction projects. At the end of our last release in Kielder Forest in 2022, we were pleased to hand over our pre-loved release pens to friends from the Eden Rivers Trust who hoped to use them for a future release in Cumbria. So I was delighted recently to see local and national press coverage of the release of water voles on the RSPB Haweswater Reserve and in the neighbouring Lowther Estate. In the last decade there has been a growing realisation that we need to be ever more active in the restoration of our wild countryside. Releases of water voles, beaver; osprey, golden eagle and harvest mice are some of the exciting examples. But to enable these to be successful there has to be much more. Ecosystems which support these glorious animals have to be restored or created. They have to be managed and balance restored as far as possible. It is sad but necessary for some species to be controlled. Red and roe deer populations have been getting out of hand. Either through intentional overstocking to support the shooting industry or the lack of natural predators. In some areas grey squirrels are driving out or infecting with squirrel pox the native red squirrel population. And mink are eating our water voles! We have created these imbalances and if we want to see the restoration and expansion of our native wildlife we need to intervene. Maybe one day we will see the successful reintroduction or increase of some of our native apex predators such as the lynx and the wolf, but I can't see this being possible on a large-enough scale on our small island. We therefore need to invest in our wild if we want to keep and grow it. Not through short term over managed projects which create some tenuous political gains, but through long term and consistent investment.

Marvellous and successful as our water vole releases have been, we need to see much, much more of the same.

Chapter 8

Neville Away!

Phase 3. The First Release. June 2017
So, now we are all set and ready to go. About time too. It's Chapter 8 already and we haven't released any voles yet. Get on with it. Here we go.

Nervous energy abounded. And some biscuits. Neville and our first batch of volunteer water voles were en route from South Devon accompanied by Derek and his expert crew. We needed to be ready. Kelly and Graham had a detailed plan. Suitable release areas had been identified, a team of volunteers and NWT staff would be assisted by FC partners. Release pens were ready for assembly. Refreshments had been sourced and laid out at the depot in Kielder to make sure that no-one experienced an energy gap.
So, how does this release business work? Do we just open the van door and let them out to find their own salvation? Might be a bit risky if we want most of them to survive and breed. Instead, we would follow Derek Gow's advice and do it their way. Here's how it went:

Day 1. Derek's team select a group of pioneer voles for the trip north. I hope they were given some good advice on what to expect. Compared to the luxury of their Devon home they were going to find some cool weather and encounter lots of nasty predators. More on these later. Was this good news for Neville? As a fit and healthy specimen, he was selected for the first wave of 317 voles in June. A further 243 would follow in August that year. This two-phase release was repeated for the next five years. The official report lists 2089 voles released by the end of 2021. A further 200+ were released in 2022 as the result of a further donation.

Day 2. The journey north. Neville and his companions were put into their comfortable travel pods with plenty of straw and food for the journey. It's a journey of several hundred miles. Each of these boxes would contain either a family group of mother and kits, a male and female matched by the team as a likely couple or a single vole. The latter usually an older vole which would probably be released before the rest. At the end of their long road trip, they arrive at the Forestry Commission depot in Kielder Village where they are fed and housed before being checked and put to bed by the team. We were lucky with all of our twelve releases that the weather wasn't too hot. There is always the danger on a long journey in an enclosed van that voles would suffer and possibly die from the heat. If that had been a risk the deliveries would have been postponed.

Kelly gives a pep talk to the newly arrived voles as they prepare for a good night's sleep in their travel pods.

The pens are filled with straw for bedding

These release pens come flat packed. A bit like IKEA but without the instructions. There are hinges all over. At each end the door will open outwards and then the whole thing collapses. Mind your fingers. You'll notice that at one end there are sheets of blue or white plastic covering the wire. This provides shelter for the living quarters where the straw has been placed for Neville's comfort. Some voles leave it there, others spread it all over the pen. We occasionally get some warm sunny days, in fact lots of them during release season. To make sure the voles don't overheat, the exposed half of the pen is covered with some local brash – small branches and vegetation – to provide shade. To fit the baffle board on Day 3, the door at the top, as we look at it here, is opened and the board is tied over the opening. The pen is lying flat at that stage of course. Neville and his friends are then free to leave when they choose

Day 3. The team are out early preparing the release sites. The streams are explored for suitable spots for release – relatively still water, plenty of vegetation cover, stream banks with potential for burrowing. The release pens are assembled. Carrots and apples are being cut for the first day's repast. One piece of each per vole. Meanwhile Rachel and Coral from Derek's team are checking that the voles are still in their crates, a few have been known to chew their way out and run around in the shed but none have been lost at this stage. Just more stress for the crew. And the press are expected for this first release so the make-up crew are also busy.

Then the voles are transported to the release site. Sounds simple, but some of these are pretty remote and the trip involves several kilometres on forest tracks. "Which way were we supposed to turn here?" "Turn left just beyond the block of trees." "Which bloody trees? There's millions of them. It's a forest!"

Eventually the site is reached. Some of the crew are there waiting, getting more excited with every biscuit.

After arriving at the site, the team have a planning meeting and specific tasks are allocated. "You're on the baffle boards (I'll explain these later), you're filling the pens with straw, you're putting in the feed, you're carrying the pens out to the stream, you're helping transfer the voles into the pens." Sometimes people stuck to their task but generally we all just mucked in. And everyone wanted to help with - or watch – the transfer of these real, wild creatures into the pens. They are beautiful creatures. Furry, dark chestnut to black and full of excitement. This was the time to get a real close up look at the animals, to take photos, maybe get the chance to transfer them into the release pen and give them a name. Well, maybe not the latter as I was to come to regret.

Then the voles are carefully removed from their crates, one at a time so that they can be checked over to ensure they're fit for release. You may have come across the use of a tubular cardboard package which once held a particular brand of snack for this purpose. You may notice one in the pictures. No sponsorship has been provided by this company, so please try to ignore the label. Nevertheless, volunteers were usually willing to help to empty these tubes in preparation for the event. How selfless of them. To persuade the voles to participate in the transfer they have been placed into a large circular plastic container like the ones you might use for garden waste. Their straw has been added at the same time so that they feel safe. Then the said cardboard tube is lowered to the bottom of the bin and the vole can be coaxed to enter it, mistaking the tube for a burrow perhaps. They're just the right size. Once the vole is in the tube its tail will usually be seen protruding from it. By gently, but firmly taking hold of the tail the vole can be manoeuvred back to the mouth of the tube and here it will cling. Now in full view the vole can be inspected, checked for health and gender – don't want to make any mistakes there – and then gently lowered into its new, temporary home. Once the pen has its full allocation of voles, anything from two to seven, the number is written on the pen so that sufficient food can be added next day. The pen is closed securely and two members of the team carry it carefully to the point of release. This sounds straightforward but often involved a trip of several hundred metres across very rough terrain. You need a break after a couple of these trips. And Kelly had thoughtfully supplied a range of drinks and snacks, as well as midge repellent and sun cream – yes, even in Kielder Forest the sun may shine.

Surprisingly, perhaps, no volunteers or staff have been harmed during these releases. Apart from the mental stress caused by carrying so much responsibility and mixing with so many naturalists. They're a great and varied bunch.

Then it's time for a tidy up, a return to base for a de-brief and planning for the next day. Whilst the voles rest peacefully in their secure temporary holiday homes the team return home for a "warm bath, massage, meal and glass or two of wine" – sorry I just fell into a dream state there. Usually it was a quick wash, fall asleep on the settee and wake up in the night with nightmares about American mink. Meanwhile Derek and his team were ensconced in the nearby hostelry beguiling the locals with tales of Dartmoor ponies and wild cats.

Wendy and Sue approach their baffle board on the North Tyne. Catcleugh Field, Kielder Village, where several American mink had been apprehended. You can see the baffle board lying in the grass. Marking the spot where the pen should be placed.

Day 4. You probably thought that was it. No. Only half the voles had been put out in their pens on Day 3. Now these had to fed – one piece of carrot and apple each, you remember. And this involved the same journey of course. In the vans and off through the forest until the site was reached. Then, buckets of food in hand, the long or short walk over rough ground to reach the release pens. A bit of logistical thinking is needed here. Have you got enough food in your bucket to supply all of the pens? If you haven't and you started feeding at the nearest pen you may find you run out of food several hundred yards away from base. And you know what the terrain is like. Now you have a dilemma. Leave the voles to starve or face walking all the way back to the van, replenishing the bucket and making a second long journey. You know what you have to do. If you'd started by walking out to the furthest pen, with a full bucket admittedly, by the time you'd run out of food you would be almost back at the van and had only a short trip to make. You might even persuade someone else to do it seeing as all they've been doing is watching Coral unload the voles. Not that I ever made this mistake, of course. Anyway, you're here now, check the number of voles in each pen. This was written on the pen when the voles were put in yesterday. Each vole then provided with the specified food – apple and carrot again – which had to be carefully placed into the pen without leaving a gap for adventurous voles to escape through. I can only recall one vole achieving this and disappearing off into the undergrowth. That one probably got first choice of a nice new burrow site. Whilst this was being done, Coral and Rachel were preparing the second batch of voles for release and the whole process was repeated on the new sites. Could you run me through that again?

Sue checks out a healthy-looking specimen who looks to see if there's anything left in the tube. Too late, Graham got there first.

Meanwhile the Ratty van waits to transport the next cohort to their new home.

Day 5. Well that first batch of voles from Day 3 were getting restless. They had been given time to familiarise themselves with the sights and sounds and smells of a Kielder day and night. No doubt some pens had been visited by interested members of the surrounding riverbank community. Not all with good intentions. Time for some burrowing. All of the pens were now out and all needed fresh food delivered. More trekking across those treacherous stretches of hillside.

And for the Day 3 voles, a special surprise and an opportunity for freedom. Their pens were fitted with "baffle boards". Remember them? The baffle board fits across one end of the release pen and has two water vole-size holes in it. One at each side. These holes are large enough to allow the voles out or in but too small for large predators such as fox or otter. And if a stoat or weasel gets in the voles have the second hole to escape through. We have never found any sign of voles being predated in the pen. The baffle boards are left in place for two days to give the voles time to make up their minds about when to leave their new home. Their response is interesting. On several occasions voles have bolted through the holes almost as the board was being fitted. One even ran across Sue's foot as she stood by the pen. The voles then instinctively head for cover; in the dense vegetation or into the stream and under the overhanging banks. Usually, but not always, they're quickly out of sight. However, most voles bide their time. Probably waiting until we large creatures are out of the way before tentatively poking their noses out deciding to leave. Several pleasant lunch breaks have been spent sitting on the stream banks and watching as voles left the pens and explored the area. Some immediately digging burrows to get out of danger, others wandering off along the stream sides.

Day 6. All the voles have to be fed again, even those which had the baffle boards fitted yesterday. Just in case some shy bairns are still in the pen. And now the Day 4 vole pens had to be baffled. I bet you are by now.

Day 7. Just the Day 4 voles to be fed today. A pleasant drive in the forest. Relaxing in the sun, lunch by the stream swatting away the midges. Staring at those holes in the baffle boards. Hoping to see a new Neville. (No, I've told you not to give them names anymore!) Usually just a couple of us after an easy day and finished by lunch time. No paella allowed.

Day 8. One of the hardest and least popular days. Collecting in, dismantling and storing all those now empty pens. Only once have a found a live vole still in its pen on the second day after the baffle was fitted. And once a dead one. Not bad considering we have released in the region of 2,200 voles. Some of the release pens are a bit battered by now and in need of some TLC. So Graham goes off to set a date for some maintenance days when repairs can be made. Learning as you go along is how most things improve, isn't it. In subsequent years we planned these maintenance days a week or so before the next release. That meant there wouldn't be any forgotten tasks or deterioration over the winter. Pens could be renovated, cleaned and even taken out to the new site well in advance of the new arrivals.

And so our first release was done. Wow. A real sense of achievement shared by everyone, I think. 320 water voles had been set free in nine different locations, mainly to the north-east of Kielder Village and not too far off the Forest Drive. The two main sites were along the Kielder and Scaup burns. (See map of release sites below.) The majority of the voles were released via the slow-release method using release pens as seen above. About 50 lone individuals which hadn't been paired up had been put out via "hard release". This is when the travel pod (I much prefer that name to plastic crate) they had arrived in is taken to a suitable spot by a stream and opened up so that they can leave immediately and start to explore their new "'hood". I am always struck by how individual their reactions to this are. A minority of voles spring straight from the pod, dive into the stream or disappear into the undergrowth, barely giving their releaser time to see where they've gone. More often they'll take a bit of time. Sticking their nose out to sniff the air, have a look around, go back under the straw to think about it before cautiously exiting and seeking cover. A smaller number are very reluctant to leave. Sensing the presence of humans, they bury themselves into the straw and simply refuse to move until a gentle push from behind, or the removal of their straw blanket persuades them they'd be better off outside. And off they go. Most voles are soon hidden in the undergrowth or hiding under the overhanging banks of the stream. But a few are more adventurous, or foolhardy. On the first release described above, reporters and camera crew from BBC Look North were in attendance, wanting some good shots.

The release site chosen was at a large pond on the Scaup Burn which would give us the best chance of seeing a vole swimming off into the sunset. Most of the voles chose not to co-operate and went straight for the safety of the lush vegetation around the pond. But then one would-be celebrity vole decided he/she needed the publicity and struck off across the pond in full view of the camera and cheering onlookers. Finally, after a few heart-stopping minutes the performer reached the far bank, glanced over her/his shoulder and disappeared into the safety of the reeds where they needed to be. The risk was undoubtedly reduced by the number of humans present, thus deterring any would-be predator. Herons frequent the pond and nearby there is a tawny owl nest. And we know that tawny owls love a vole feast, normally the smaller field and bank voles but they have been known to take the much larger water vole. Owl pellets found in the area since the release have shown water vole remains to be present. Can they really swallow something so large? Or do they need to divide it up into more manageable portions? Anyway, the BBC were delighted to see the antics of our new celeb and I suspect they may have offered it a contract. And I continue to be amazed that an animal born and raised in an enclosure in Devon, with no access to water deep enough to swim in, can instinctively head straight for the deep water and swim across such a pond, or a fast-flowing stream. And with such nonchalance.

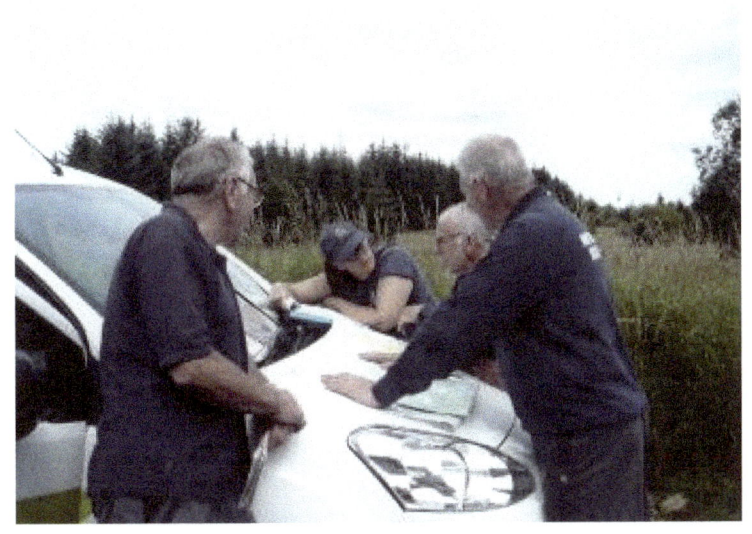

"Do all volunteers have grey hair?", thought Neville. Looks like they're lost. Consulting my trusty OS map, see below. (Don, Kelly, Mel & Dave)

Chapter 9

Company for Neville

Phase 4. Release and Monitor for Four More Years. 2017 -2021
It was only originally meant to be two more years of release, but good publicity and a growing public concern and support brought forward some additional funding which allowed for a further two years of breeding and releasing. Leading to the final release of well over 2,000 voles in total. Where were we going to put them all? Above is the rather tattered OS Map which I have carried with me from the start. On it I tried to mark the location of all of the mink monitoring rafts, trail cameras and release sites. It was good enough for the purposes of us volunteers but has a few omissions. Graham's official maps are shown later. They contain the true facts.

The OS map also proved useful for finding our way around the forest. A suitable use for a map, as I'm sure you'll agree. Relying upon satnav or mobile phone signals up in the wild lands of Kielder Forest isn't usually a good idea, as a couple of examples will illustrate.

Tall tale 1. Which way to Edinburgh?
Janet was up early that morning. She had a long trip and a full day ahead. She was due in Edinburgh in the afternoon with a brief call to make on the way in the Tyne Valley. Being February it was still dark outside and the weather forecast wasn't great. Mostly cloudy with some rain. Living in a Manchester suburb she was quite used

to this. After a quick breakfast and some time putting on her new business suit, bought last week in Hobbs - class will tell you know - she was pleased to settle into her new gleaming-white company car and off she set. The route to the Tyne Valley was familiar and from there she had the new car's satnav to get her to Edinburgh. The journey went well and the first bit of business was soon settled very much to her satisfaction. Now she made her first mistake. Not being very familiar with satnav, she entered the "short route" option and off she set. As she drove north the landscape became quite hilly and the roads quite narrow. It had begun to rain steadily. As she passed through a little town called Bellingham the rain began to turn to sleet, but it soon stopped and she could admire the expanse of a large lake off to her right. The road was getting quite narrow now and she was directed to turn right through the rather unusual little settlement which was Kielder Village with its strange castle. Then she came to a right turn but there was a barrier across her half of the road and a notice saying that this was the Forest Drive. But the other lane was clear and satnav confidently told her to carry on and so she did. Now she began to get a bit concerned. Time was getting on and progress on this little road was a bit slow. And then the tarmac started to run out and she found herself on a gravel track. Could this be right? Satnav said so and on she went. And the sleet was falling again now. This must have distracted her because where the Forest Drive turned sharply right, she went straight on, across a very narrow bridge with a little stone sign that read "Stanley Cross". She wasn't too happy herself by this time, but she carried on, with the number of potholes she had to deal with just making the stress worse. At last she spotted a farmhouse ahead but there was no-one around and the track ran out. Now she really was worried. She must have missed a turn somewhere. All she could do was turn around and retrace her steps. And her new white car was getting a bit muddy. As she wondered where she had missed her turn, she saw headlights approaching and a black four-wheel drive which turned confidently up a track leading off to her right. That must be the right way and so she followed. But the track kept rising and the sleet was threatening to turn to snow. After what seemed like several miles, but which in fact was only about one, the vehicle ahead pulled off into a large lay-by alongside a pond. The track ahead disappeared into a thick area of forest and was rising even more. By now Janet was in a state of panic. She couldn't risk carrying on and so she pulled in alongside the black Mitsubishi L200. Was this a safe thing to do she asked herself. There was some strange writing on the L200. Beneath the thick layer of mud, she could make out "Northumberland Wildlife Trust". Was this some local group who liked to enjoy themselves? Would she be safe? Before she could do any more, the driver's door opened and out stepped a large man clad in dark waterproof clothing. He approached the car with a look on his face which she couldn't decipher. She grabbed her mobile phone and decided to ring the office. No signal! OK, nothing else for it. She wound down the window. "'Ello, 'Ello, 'Ello! What have we 'ere?" said the man. (This was Don. He's an ex-police officer. Used to be police driver so he could turn out to be useful.) He was soon joined by a smaller but equally bedraggled colleague. "Are you alright?" he said, "we wondered why you were following us." They were volunteers who had stopped to check something called a mink raft. In this weather – I know they must be mad. Janet burst into tears. When she had calmed down and explained what had happened the crew offered to show her the way out of the forest once they had checked the raft. Much relieved Janet noticed two other figures crouching in the back of the L200. Neither of them seemed very keen on getting out and helping Don and his friend Mel. Who can blame them?

Don and Mel did their job and offered to lead Janet back to the A68 so that she could carry on to Edinburgh. She shouldn't be too late for her meeting and the sleet was easing off. "You must be joking", she exclaimed. "Show me the way back to Manchester, I'm f…….. off home." I think that was some sort of business jargon.

It was just as well that she did meet us because if she had carried on along the Forest Drive she would eventually have come to a locked barrier just before the track emerged onto the A68.

This is a true story - mostly. Don and I did meet a lady in a white car in the sleet/snow in the valley of the Scaup Burn. And she was on her way to Edinburgh. I may have embroidered the rest of the story a bit.

Don't always trust your satnav. Earlier versions did think the Forest Drive was a public road. Some may still do.

Tall tale 2. Let's Go Camping.

On a Monday afternoon a couple of years later Sue and I were driving through the forest on the other side of Kielder Water, heading back towards Kielder Dam after checking a couple of rafts. As we approached a junction and I swung to the right - slowly of course - Sue spotted some logs across the end of the other track. "Stop" she said. "I think those logs were spelling SOS!" Sure enough they were. Sue is seldom wrong. Very good at spotting vole droppings too. Anyway, we decided we couldn't ignore this and set off in the direction of a little arrow made of twigs. After a few hundred yards we found two forestry workers leaning on their van, one of them speaking on his radio. Across the track stood two disconsolate looking young men, glancing occasionally at their Audi car as it sat there in the bog. Apparently, they had borrowed the car from one of their fathers and decided to go camping in Kielder Forest for the weekend. As they approached Kielder Dam, they noticed the barrier across the track into the forest was up, so they turned in there. After driving for a few pleasant miles through the forest, taking whichever turn took their fancy they spotted a nice flat green patch of grass (sphagnum moss - oh no!) on which to camp, and turned in. Soon they were struck by a gradual sinking feeling and found that they couldn't open the doors. Scrambling out through the windows they could see that the car was sunk to the chassis with no way of getting it out. This was Saturday morning. We had come across them at 2.00pm on the Monday. Why didn't they phone for help? No phone signal. Check the map and walk out to get help. No map. OK. One of them set out to get help whilst the other stayed with the car. Several hours later he returned having walked in one or more circles before finding himself back at the car. So they settled down to wait for help. Not many people work in the forest at the weekend. Help of sorts arrived on Monday afternoon. The Forestry workers might have been able to pull the Audi out of the mire, but they're not allowed to because of the insurance risk. And even if we were kind enough to do so, we had no means of towing them out. What the foresters could do was radio the office and get someone there to arrange for a commercial recovery firm to come out and save the day. The first two companies contacted firmly declined the offer of the job. "In the middle of Kielder Forest! In a bog? You must be joking." Finally, a saviour was found and late on Monday they were evacuated to safety. The vehicle recovery cost them almost £800 before the cost of any damage to the car and the wrath of their parent. Still, they were safe. Poor lambs! Nice weekend?

Don't go out without a map.

Enough of these tallish tales. Let's get on with the story. Where were the next lot of voles going to be rehoused? 240 more voles were promised. Derek's voles were breeding well down in sunny Devon. Down there a healthy female might produce five litters in the year, averaging five in a litter with no chance of predation this makes her pretty productive. We hoped most of them would be that handsome dark chestnut to black in colour given their northern heritage.

We didn't want this population to be too far from the first release but we did have to accept that finding suitable release sites was not always easy in the rather rough and challenging terrain of Kielder Forest. The customary wisdom is that the voles should be released alongside suitable streams with good earthen banks. This gives them a routeway for escape and for movement to new territories, and would also provide them with appropriate burrowing sites. At the same time there should be ample and varied vegetation for them to feed on and to provide cover from predators. However, many, if not most of Kielder's burns and streams can be quite challenging. As this is a high and steep-sided catchment area, rainfall is often heavy and run-off rapid and very variable. Streams will rise suddenly, undercutting banks and destroying potential homes whilst stream beds are often boulder-strewn and turbulent. It's not like living on a Hampshire chalk stream or a Lincolnshire drainage dyke you know. Our voles would need to be adaptable and we think they have been. More on this when we get to surveying. Nevertheless, we found a few sites. First of all, Cheese Sike and a small tributary of Plashetts Burn were to receive about 40 voles each. These small and well-hidden streams might do well. Close to the reservoir and relatively low-lying, both were part of the Plashetts catchment. Plashetts has proven to be an interesting release site, partly because of its proximity to the Lakeside Way, a public footpath and cycleway which completely encircles Kielder Reservoir. It's a popular route and used annually for a marathon race around the lake, just the right distance. I'm not sure marathons are all that popular or sensible, having taken part in a few in my younger days. I'm still suffering the backlash, physically and mentally. Ask the rest of the team. Some people have been known to cheat - I know! - and catch the bus down the west bank. He was reported and disqualified. Anyway, the mink monitoring raft which we've had here from the start of the project began to show signs of water vole activity soon after the release. By activity I mean tracks on the clay in the raft basket and droppings (poo) on the raft itself and on the clay. And these signs have continued every year since. We've also had several reports of sightings from visitors - not marathon runners though, they're too focussed on the pain. So, there's good evidence that we have a sustainable population in this catchment.

The Bothy at Wainhope.

Our other new sites were at Wainhope, close to an occasionally visited bothy,* (see above) and at Ridge End Burn. Two interesting sites. Wainhope looks perfect for voles. The stream is on a relatively gentle gradient, although it still has significant flooding events when in spate. The banks are of very suitable material for burrowing and there is a wealth of suitable vegetation. And yet soon after the release we stopped finding signs of the voles either on the rafts or during surveys. Had all 70 or so of them been predated or died over the first winter? Several foxes had been seen snooping around the area. Or had they migrated to more promising pastures. We know that voles can move several kilometres from the release site although this is usually just the odd maverick male looking for new territory. And then surprisingly we began to capture images of water voles swimming in the Wainhope Burn several years later. Had the original population been there all along, hiding in the swampy areas away from the main stream and its violent flow? This would tally with what we believe has been happening at other sites. Or had a new population arrived? In any case they have been appearing on camera for the last 2 years so we seem to have some residents here.

There are several bothys in the forest. Mainly belonging to Forestry England. Most of these are former farmers' or shepherds' cottages and are found in fairly remote parts of the forest. They are now "maintained" for the use of walkers or cyclists looking for a very basic overnight stop. Most have a wood-fuelled stove to cook on and a few sticks of very basic furniture. Maybe some mats to lie on. The bothy version of en suite is a spade. Find your own spot and cover it up after a dip in the stream. Unfortunately, some of these havens have been closed on occasion following acts of vandalism or/and misuse. So, if you're planning on using one it's best to check in advance to see if they are open.

And at Ridge End Burn another interesting site. This one is at quite a high elevation alongside the Forest Drive as it approaches the summit at Blakehope Nick. We released most of the voles along the main stream; pretty angry when in spate; and a smaller number up along a very small feeder stream. Since then, signs of the voles are difficult to find along the main Ridge End Burn but tracks and poo have been found on the mink raft at regular intervals for six years now along the tributary stream. And surveys in the stream reveal lots of latrines and some burrows. Another sustainable population we hope, even in these conditions and with the severity of the weather up here. I have read that mink are rarely seen above the 300-metre contour, so these voles should be safe from mink. But then there's the fox, heron, buzzard, tawny owl, stoat….

Also at Blakehope Nick is a man-made feature which we first noticed appearing back in 2019. A previously existing information board was being replaced by a strange wooden structure. "That's a strange place to put a bus shelter" muttered one of the team. As it gradually took shape over the next months, we learned that it was one of a number of architectural structures to be found scattered around the forest. Some are the works of artists and sculptors; others are the work of architecture students at Newcastle University who have used a number of opportunities in the area to hone their planning and construction skills. Other structures which are worth a look can be found at the Skyspace, close to the Dark Sky Observatory, the Hollow Head, which you can climb inside, the Janus Chairs and the bird hide at Bakethin.

During these early releases we began to rationalise the way we carried out the process. What we had been taught was based on releases in areas of the country that were probably a little more forgiving in terms of terrain and access. After the first year we started to reconsider. Carrying the release pen, complete with straw, voles and their rations over very demanding land was difficult. There were numerous trips and falls as we navigated our way across land which had been ploughed for planting - very deep furrows - and subsequently felled. After the felling of the mature trees the land was covered with tree stumps and the debris of unwanted branches. Vegetation quickly grew and hid many of these obstacles which became very slippy when wet. As we fell forwards or tottered back, our main concern was not to upset the passengers. Would the voles be traumatised by the various falls or the bad language used by some volunteers as they sank up their waist in foul smelling mud? "Don't drop the voles!", was the mantra. Not, "Are you OK?". Falls were most common for the person at the rear who couldn't see where their feet were landing. Their language was often quite unacceptable. Which reminds of the day when the media were present and filming the process. On this occasion John and I had carefully performed a release journey for the camera, completing it with few stumbles or accidents. As we returned from our 400 metre trek the cameraman commented that it had looked very good on film but he'd missed a bit of the journey. Could we possibly go back and do it again? You may add your own response at this point. Keep it clean. We tried to.

After much discussion and several trials, we decided it would be easier to take the empty pens out to the release point first. Often an experienced pioneer volunteer - maybe even a member of staff if they could tear themselves away from important discussions - would act as trailblazer, exploring the best way to negotiate the terrain and dropping off baffle boards at points along the stream which looked right for the voles; i.e. water that wasn't fast flowing, earthen banks suitable for burrowing, long vegetation for cover and breakfast. A vole's idea of the perfect home. The recommended distance between release pens is 20 metres but we had to take this as a very rough guide as suitable spots were few and far between at times, and close together elsewhere. Following these brave pioneers would come the back-up brigade carrying the empty release pens, using whatever carrying technique suited them. Wendy, a frequent volunteer during release weeks, devised various pieces of useful equipment to help with this, usually made from odd bits and pieces she found around the place. Well, it sometimes worked for her.

Once on site the release pens were then put together using self-assembly techniques similar to IKEA furniture. Most of them held up reasonably well. Next came the straw carriers who would seek to find the release pens - not always as easy as it sounds in this tall vegetation and lumpy landscape - and introduce the prescribed amount of bedding material. And then the triumphal progress of the vole carriers and Coral + the food providers. Carrying the voles out in their travel pods was much easier than when they were already in the pens. It was the work of one person not two. Then, on site, Coral could check the voles and place them in the pens whilst the caterers provided the correct amounts of their five-a-day diet. This technique proved to be much easier, even though it sounds more complicated. Just a deconstructed version of the recommended method.

And then all of the releases were done. Over six years we had released twelve cohorts of voles over a wide area of the forest. I was privileged to have helped out on ten of these. The other two happened during the Covid lockdown summer when volunteers weren't allowed out in the forest. NWT and FC staff had to cope on their own. It was very stressful for them but they coped. Now we just had to carry on with checking the mink rafts once every fortnight, providing maintenance and replacement for them where necessary - and also a new task. Now we'd have to start checking on our new population of voles by carrying out regular surveys.

Using the new release method Coral checks the voles are present and correct. Don looks on as Tom practises the ritual release dance.

Meanwhile Sue tries to hide in her hoodie whilst Ken and Sharon fit a baffle board.

Chapter 10

Where's Neville?

> *"All along the backwater,*
> *Through the rushes tall,*
> *Ducks are a-dabbling,*
> *Up tails all!"*
> **(Kenneth Grahame: Wind in the Willows")**

Bottoms up for a Water Vole Survey.
If you're passing by a stream or burn in Kielder Forest and you see three bottoms sticking up in the air, spaced at regular intervals upstream don't worry. They're probably just conducting a water vole survey. There will often be one character standing on the bankside on the pretext that they are looking for signs of feeding or burrows just away from the stream. The real reason is that they conveniently "forgot" their wellies or waders because they didn't want to have to contend with cold water, slippery rocks and incessant midges. Sounds fun, doesn't it? Some people even volunteer to do this.

Well, we needed to know whether or not our voles had survived and if they were appearing elsewhere. After the first release we did find water vole prints on a mink raft on the other side of the reservoir and some eight miles from the release site. This was extreme, but we have come across sightings, latrines and tracks in areas well away from points of release.

When one reads the guidance on water vole surveys the conventional wisdom is that this is best done by following a chosen watercourse upstream. This avoids disturbed sediment and waves preceding you down the stream, hiding some of the evidence and warning voles of your approach. Preferably with at least one surveyor in the water, depth of water permitting and following all Health & Safety guidance of course. But you don't really need your 25-metre swimming badge in the burns we were in. On one occasion I was deeply absorbed in looking for signs in the stream at Cheeseburn when I got the distinct feeling that I was not alone. Taking care to rise very slowly from my crouching position, which I realised had made me invisible to anyone around, I came face to face with a roebuck. Just a couple of metres away. We stared into one another's eyes in wonder. He probably wondered what the hell was this strange object with a Tilley hat balanced on top and two eyes looking in his direction as the body slowly emerged. I wondered if he might be thinking of using those horns for some aggressive purpose. Fortunately, after several long seconds he turned his back and loped off into the forest. I was very jealous. The very thought of loping on this terrain seems impossible. Getting back to the point, if Neville or any of his type are about, you may find various signs of their presence:

A. Best of all you'll catch sight of a water vole. Often scurrying through the vegetation, hugging the side of the stream or, classically "plopping" into the water as you approach. This plopping is a very clear memory from my childhood in Lincolnshire where the banks of the myriad drainage ditches were like Vole City. As you walked along the top of the bank (or bund) you would hear the plop and look up to see a small head making its' way across the drainage channel leaving a clear V shape in its wake. And then another, and another and so on. They were so common that after a while it made no impression. Little did we expect that this lovely creature with its key role in the balance of the ecosystem would be almost vanished within a few decades. Careless youth, eh! Anyway, back to now. We did get the occasional plop, but not many as our little streams were a bit rocky and not very ploppable. Is that a new word? I do recall standing with Dave and peering over the bridge on the Plashetts Burn as a large, very black vole munched away on the vegetation on the bank, seemingly oblivious to our presence. On another occasion at March Sike I was in the stream busily checking the mink raft when there was a plop behind me. No crude comments please. The rest of the team shouted out in glee "a vole, a vole, we've seen a vole, hurray!" All very Enid Blyton, I thought. As I turned to see it, I saw only the ripples. Foiled again. Often the mink rafts have been as good a source of water vole evidence as the surveys. The two have to be taken together as evidence, I think. Trail cameras too. We began to deploy these after the first couple of years and they have thrown up lots of interesting pictures, apart from water voles - the most exciting being the pine marten, which has become more frequent over the last three years. Otters were common too, but never mink, which tends to lead to the conclusion that they aren't that common around the forest. Images of water voles have not been common on our cameras. They seem to have a way of avoiding them although they do appear occasionally. Having another source of data is very useful as we had found at Wainhope, near the bothy.

B. Latrines and poo. The next best thing I'm sure you'll agree. "Poo, poo, I've found poo" shouts Sue. Quite a frequent sound as Sue is undoubtedly our best poo detective. They are almost entirely vegetarian; although female voles (not Sue) are known to eat caddis fly larva, crayfish and small fresh water shrimps when they're pregnant. They need to top up their protein levels. Not surprising if you're producing up to 30 or so offspring in the year. Water voles produce poo which is not unpleasant to smell. Especially when compared with mink poo which absolutely reeks. Sorry, mink, nothing personal. The poo is dark green to black in colour and capsule shaped, rounded at both ends and similar in size and shape to a Tic Tac mint. But water vole poo isn't white and you shouldn't eat it. When the poo is broken apart it crumbles easily to reveal lots of vegetative remains. No bones, skin or fur which you might find in the droppings of a rat, fox or pine marten. Water voles will deposit their poo randomly around their territory and even in the water. On a visit to colleagues in the North Yorkshire Moors, one of their members of staff stooped in the stream as soon as we arrived and scooped a single dropping from the surface of the water. He said they were easy to spot and common. I think he had maybe brought it along in his pocket just to impress. But more importantly and useful for determining the presence and territory of the voles are the latrines.

These are piles of poo, added to over time to mark out the territory. These are most easy to find along the course of the stream, usually slightly hidden under the bank on a muddy pile or a convenient boulder just above the water line. Back in North Yorkshire we found several latrines out in the open on top of hummocks of sphagnum moss. I've never seen that in Kielder Forest. I suspect this would make the vole too exposed to the attentions of all those predators. But I don't know why those Yorkshire voles would be so brazen. Are there fewer predators about? Finding a fresh latrine is very clear evidence that we have a vole population in the area. Sometimes the latrine seems to have been slightly flattened and the individual droppings squashed together and out of shape. This can make the latrine a bit harder to spot but is a good sign as it indicates that a male vole has visited the latrine and is marking his presence, probably adding some of his own droppings to the pile. But latrines are definitely our second favourite sign of water vole presence. And I've never seen a vole in the act of creating a latrine. It wouldn't be polite to look, would it?

C. Burrows. This is where they live when they're not out grazing or looking for a mate. Most of the literature will tell you that these burrows will tend to be along the streamside. They usually have one entrance under the water level, enabling them to escape from predators by diving and entering their tunnel underwater, and another on top of the bank above water level to prevent the burrow from flooding when there is high water. Having at least two entrances also increases your chances of escape should a female mink or a stoat intrude. Beneath the surface there will be a network of tunnels and chambers where the voles can sleep, rear their young and store their food. This is where we may have a problem in Kielder Forest. Burrows have been quite difficult to find in the expected places but have been stumbled upon well away from the water courses. This makes them a lot more difficult to find. It's easy to follow a burn upstream but when the whole land area becomes the potential habitat where do you look? The ground in the forest is very rough and uneven. Simply walking across it can be a significant challenge. But we do find burrows and burrow systems, even if not as often as we'd like. Very occasionally we would come across what seemed to be a burrow entrance but this was blocked with fresh earth or clay. Apparently, this is a sign that there are kits inside the burrow and the mother has blocked the entrance to prevent predators from entering the burrow system.

D. Feeding signs. Voles like to forage around an area and collect piles of food for later consumption or storage. Their bite is quite distinctive and leaves a cut edge across the blade of grass, sedge or whatever at a 45-degree angle. So vole feeding signs are quite easy to identify. But what sort of vole is it? Field voles and bank voles leave the same pattern of bite. But they are significantly smaller animals and their feed stores are of a shorter length than the water vole, being around 3-4cm long compared to the water voles' 8-10cm. In other areas voles may create grazed lawns around the entrance to the burrow.

What did all this surveying reveal? The first thing I would note was the resilience and patience of the volunteers and their leaders. And some of their survival skills. Some days were very exciting with lots of evidence of water voles. Poo latrines galore and nice fresh burrows. Very occasionally an actual vole was sighted. Most often a smaller field vole but sometimes the real thing. On these days even the midges and the odd wasp sting were tolerable. But there were also days when we found nothing. Hours of paddling upstream trying not to get a welly full. Even some very small streams have deep pools. Best to wear waders even if they do make you look silly. These days were valuable too, of course. That's citizen science for you. We needed to know where the voles were not doing well as much as we needed to know where they were. We can only speculate as to why the voles quickly disappeared from some release sites. I think it unlikely that they were all predated by herons and other culprits, although this might be the case with some of the smaller populations. More likely, and we have some evidence of this, is that they found conditions around the streams to be too challenging. Moving away from the stream sides the land is often very boggy, crossed by tiny drainage channels and with lots of tall vegetation. Surveying these often-extensive areas is extremely difficult. However, on a number of occasions on finishing our surveys and trekking back to the vehicle we have come across evidence of water vole activity. Burrows and feeding signs most often. We have also found signs of water voles well away from any release area, notably on the Smales Burn in the south east of the area and right on the edge of forestry land.

But best of all are the overall survey results from 2023. A team of staff and volunteers led by Ph.D. student and integrated member of the Ratty team, Ellesse Janda, surveyed all of the areas close to release sites and further afield. Her map showing areas inhabited by water voles corresponds remarkably well with that of the release sites. It also includes populations away from these. The overall impact then appears to be very positive with water voles found throughout the catchment, and spreading. Encouraging results which show that the water vole can make a comeback if habitats are managed sensitively and the mink population is controlled, or even better eradicated. Sadly, there is no evidence yet of a slowing down in the decrease of the water vole population in the UK overall, although evidence from the mink eradication programme in East Anglia is more positive and suggests that given the chance the water vole could thrive once again on our island. Recently I read the good news that the Waterlife Recovery Trust in East Anglia have been awarded a significant grant to extend their work on mink eradication. Their new project will cover a wider area, from the Thames north to mid-Lincolnshire, whilst maintaining a presence in a buffer zone to protect the area already cleared. Great news but if their ambition is to rid the UK of mink entirely, then more will be required and a commitment to do this, dependent on its continued success, would be a positive step and an indication that funding bodies, and the government, take this issue seriously.

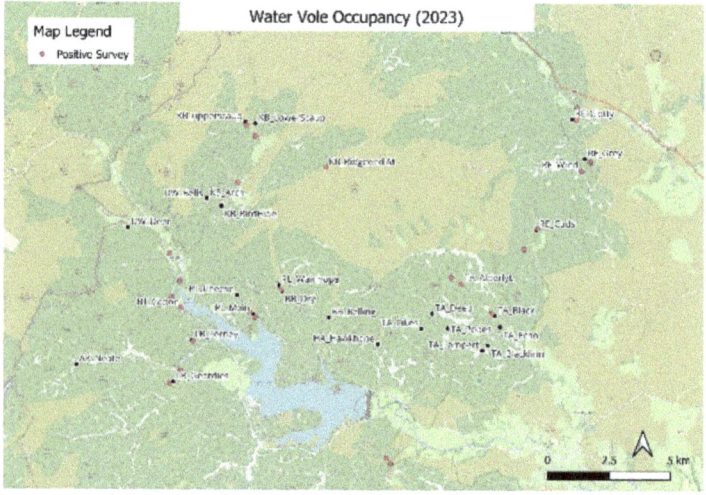

Surveys led by Ellesse Janda in 2023 show that water voles were present throughout the core release area and beyond. Indeed, the occupancy map shows a strong correlation with that of the release sites. The two dots in the south of the map are of particular interest as they show the presence of the voles well beyond the nearest release site. It would be interesting now to survey more sites away from the core release area to see if there are more such outliers.

Signs of water vole activity.

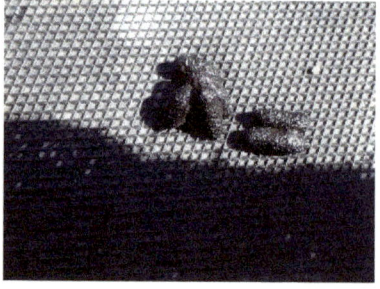

Entrance to a burrow. Occasionally found with fresh mud blocking the entrance. Indicates pregnant female and kits inside.

Vole droppings or "poo". Water vole about the size and shape of a Tic Tac. Field vole size of a grain of rice.

Feeding signs. Bitten at a 45-degree angle. 5-10 cm. long. If shorter, probably field or bank vole.

Best sign of all is to spot one. This one thinks she's hidden.

Ratty Team March On

And so for the next five years we continued with the annual cycle. The location of our mink monitoring rafts was periodically reviewed as new release sites came on stream, some locations proved unsuitable because of issues such as the volatility of a stream or access problems. But every fortnight the rafts and trail cameras needed to be checked. During the summer season, usually from March/April through to the end of September, teams would be out conducting surveys. And, most exciting were the two release weeks each year. As the area which had been re-voled expanded, we were constantly seeking out suitable release sites, occasionally resulting in some head scratching with maps out, whilst we tried to work out where we were and how to get home. And the motivation to visit some unknown locations may have been as much to do with general curiosity and the chance to explore otherwise remote parts of the forest as it did with looking for vole homes. Suddenly finding ourselves at the top of Deadwater Fell (fascinating) or outside Kielder Observatory was a pleasant surprise.

As I mentioned earlier, the mink rafts provided valuable information about animal activity in the area as well as early warning signs of mink. Fortunately, there have been only a few mink intrusions and these along predictable riparian corridors; upstream along the River North Tyne and its tributary the Tarset Burn as well as over the border from Scotland, crossing the watershed near Deadwater and, coincidentally the "Daft as a Brush" trail, which traces the course of the Tyne from source to mouth. ("Daft as a Brush" being a local charity which provides valuable support to the families of cancer patients.) Should signs of mink be detected. then the alert goes out and humane traps are set at and around the site. These traps are baited to attract the mink. Various baits have been trialled and championed by different people. Some recommend fish paste or cat food. Others, including Tim from Dundee University, recommend the scent gland from another, presumably deceased, mink. These traps must be checked twice daily to ensure that no animal is left in there for too long. The use of "smart" traps which can alert the responsible person remotely via mobile phone link can be a great time saver and more humane too as the target will be to get to the trap and check it asap. Unfortunately, the lack of a decent phone signal in the Kielder Forest area makes the use of smart technology impossible at the moment, although new satellite-driven technology promises to redress this problem soon. Any "innocent" intruders are immediately released when the trap is checked. But for the unlucky mink the outcome is less welcome. It will be despatched as quickly and humanely as possible. It is illegal to release a mink back into the wild once it has been apprehended. Or in any other circumstance.

The film crew visiting the Hollow Head on the shores of Kielder Water.

And what else have we found on or around our mink rafts? I have already referred to the use of these rafts for assisting with our water vole surveys. The voles seem to be as interested in these strange floating islands as our predators are. Some of the rafts are regularly visited by voles which leave their distinctive prints in the clay, often accompanied by a little, or a lot of poo. Suitable surfaces for latrines perhaps. This poo may be on the clay or on the outside area of the raft, more often here when it's an obvious latrine. And what else? Various small mammals, including field vole and shrew, also stoat, weasel, otter, pine marten, red and grey squirrel. And domestic cat, and brown rat. We think we had badger once; it could probably just about squeeze its front paw far enough into the housing to scratch the surface of the clay. And various small birds, difficult to identify from their feet but judging by what we see on the trail cameras probably grey wagtail, dipper and chaffinch.

Chapter 11

They Came to See Neville
I'm A Celebrity Get Me to Kielder

You're probably wondering about some of the other NWT activities which have taken place in and around Kielder Forest and Reservoir in recent years. I've alluded to them at various points along the way so let's find out a bit more. What's the connection between Kielder Forest and the humpback whale? No, there are no humpbacks in Kielder Water. As far as we know. Could we start a new Nessie rumour of our own?

The very tenuous connection is that in 2019 Daisybeck Studios in Leeds made a wildlife documentary called "Wild Animal Rescue" for Channel 5. It was streamed in 2020. Whilst the series included features from around the UK, including a kayaker's encounter with a humpback off the coast of Cornwall, much of the filming was done in Kielder Forest and so the company decided that they would do all of the continuity filming there. I told you it was tenuous. Anyway, having visited the forest to film our 2019 water vole release etc, they had lots of footage of red squirrels and ospreys as well as the voles. Now they needed to return in order to film their commentary back on site. A slight problem then occurred to them. Getting around the forest without any road signs can be tricky. Would they be able to re-find the locations? Just to be safe they asked NWT if it would be possible for someone to act as their forest guide. I was asked if I could oblige and I jumped at the chance. It was a very rewarding and interesting experience over a rather chilly week in the autumn of 2019. Forestry England were just a little concerned that the guide might get lost and so provided back up from soon-to-be retired forestry worker Dennis. We spent a very pleasant week together and, thanks to Dennis, I hardly ever got lost or lost any of the film crew.

The crew were around for a week. Each morning, we would gather early to plan the day ahead with various well-known faces showing up to do their continuity bits. It was fascinating to watch the complexity of the operation with the various roles being played by the film crew, the lighting crew, the sound crew, the directors and all the gophers etc. Once the team had sorted out the logistics, we were off to various parts of the forest with Dennis or me in the lead vehicle. I don't remember anyone getting lost and since then we have no records of coming across shell-shocked cameramen stumbling around the forest, so I think it went OK.

The simplest day for me was taking the crew to the locations where they had shot footage of our water vole release. Here we met up with the famous Kelly Hollings, our co-leader, and I was delighted to see how impressive she was in front of the camera. She's a natural and I think she got all the questions right and didn't have to do too many re-takes. Which couldn't be said for one or two of the other presenters. But I can't tell you which ones or they will probably sue me. I probably signed something forbidding me to do any such thing. But I recall one of them getting frustrated as she prepared for her twentieth take. It all looks so natural on TV.

Another favourite scene for me was watching Northumberland's own Joanna Dailey in conversation with Bill Oddie. Joanna is famous for her work with Kielder Ospreys and produces an excellent blog which has recorded the return and success of this fabulous fish eagle since its return to Kielder in 2009. This heralded the first natural return of these birds to England since the nineteenth century, although they can now be found around Rutland Water, in North Wales and on the south coast as a result of reintroduction programmes. Joanna is so attached to these birds that she often undertakes an annual migration herself, popping down to the Gambia and the Senegal river to see for herself where they spend our winter. Can't blame them, can you? I remember how delighted she was the first time she actually spotted one of the Kielder ospreys in a tree in west Africa. She knew it was a Kielder osprey because she had put a ring on it. Since their return in 2009 and the establishment of a single nest, the number of birds returning has increased each year so that we now have nine productive nests and rumours of others in sites outside of the Kielder area. This success hasn't simply happened without any assistance. Forestry England built artificial nesting platforms for the birds in order to attract them. Necessary because Sitka spruce don't offer much of an opportunity for nesting and there are very few old trees in the forest. Since then, staff and volunteers have kept a very careful eye on the nests to ensure that they are not disturbed by misguided individuals who would like to get a closer look or even steal the eggs or chicks. Joanna is a real unsung hero of the nature conservation world. Bill Oddie is quite well known too.

On another occasion Steve Backshall - yes, I know I'm doing a lot of name-dropping here, I don't get out a lot - was with us in the forest looking at the signs that pine martens are making a comeback in this extreme northerly bit of England. He did a bit of commentary about those humpback whales as well. But the exciting bit, of course, is that the pine marten does seem to be making a bit of a comeback here. When we first started in 2014 there were rumours of this iconic mustelid, some of them obviously quite historic, but others from reliable sources from residents and farmers in the area. But we saw no signs of them on the rafts or evidence of their scat as we roved around. But in 2017 on our raft at Waterhead we found prints unlike any others we had seen up to then. Sue and I were quite convinced it was pine marten but back at base they were more sceptical. Whether we were right or not, within a couple of years we were getting quite regular images of the elusive beast on the trail camera at Waterhead and later at Ridge End Burn.

And we have found probable pine marten droppings at those and other locations. Good news for red squirrels perhaps as it is thought that pine martens will prey on the grey squirrel and drive it out of the area. They will certainly take reds too but the red can escape more easily being lighter and more agile.

And whilst we are on with the name dropping, I spent a very pleasant afternoon watching Miranda Krestovnikoff filming a piece about the red squirrels outside the red squirrel hide at Leaplish Waterside Park. As Miranda was being filmed, I was strictly told not to disturb the filming. Dennis and I occasionally got a stern look from the production crew as we nattered away off-screen. The sound crew could be hypersensitive to any noises off so on this occasion I really had to control my enthusiasm. As Miranda was chatting on-screen about this lovely little mammal, one of them - we're talking squirrel now, not the production team - jumped across from a neighbouring tree and began to walk along a branch just above her head. She and the camera crew were quite oblivious to this and I was desperate to bring their attention to it. It was perfect. The animal found a nice little spot and adopted the classic squirrel pose with its fluffy tail tucked over its head. It must have been very interested in what Miranda was saying because it sat there for the whole time, never interrupting her or correcting anything she said. And as soon as she finished it was off. Probably shocked by the shout of "cut" just below it. You can't be too careful with these humans around. Ironically this star-struck squirrel never appeared on the TV. The part was probably taken by one of the professionals at Derek Gow's film school in Devon. A small part of Derek's work is providing extras for wildlife programmes. If the desired animal won't co-operate and be filmed in situ then Derek probably has a couple of examples of the genus who are willing to be filmed and enjoy their 15 minutes. I have every sympathy with the squirrel I mention above because a short interview I did for the programme about the joys of volunteering was cut at the last edit. My big chance was gone. Me and the squirrel meet up occasionally to share our bad luck stories.

Any more name dropping? Well, if you're a fan of "The Yorkshire Vet" on Channel 5 you'll be thrilled to know that Peter Wright, protégé of the great James Herriot, and his partner Julian Norton were there too. At one point as Julian was waiting for his turn, I was chatting to him about the forest and he became curious about what all these trees were for. "Well,", I said, "down in the valley is a wood pulp factory and another which makes 25% of the country's toilet rolls. You could be leaning on your next one now"

Some celebrities: Joanne & Bill; Kelly; Steve Backshall; the Isuzu

Chapter 12
What Now for Neville?

Can there be an "exit strategy"? Well, unless there is some plan for the continued monitoring of the mink population and other factors affecting the sustainability of our new water vole population there is a danger that all of the efforts of the last ten years could be in vain. We have seen too many "projects" which are supported by short term funding collapse once the funding disappears. I have seen this in my previous existence in the field of education and more recently in the world of nature conservation. Having invested so much time and emotional energy in our Restoring Ratty project I fervently hope that a real and meaningful sustainability plan can be agreed between all of the partners involved. It is my personal opinion that such a strategy will need to expand beyond the bounds of the Restoring Ratty project and with two major prongs.

First of these would be a continued effort to eradicate the population of American mink, initially within the area included in the Naturally Native project (another short-term funding project which has achieved a lot in a short time and where all that effort could be wasted if there is no follow-up and expansion of its aims) and then beyond to cover the north of England and ideally the whole of the UK and Ireland by linking with other similar initiatives.

Secondly, I believe that more should be done to reintroduce water voles to their previous home territories where, until very recently there were very healthy populations. To imagine that the Kielder population will be sufficient to ensure its long-term viability AND spread throughout the neighbouring area would be optimistic. This is particularly true given the challenging environment of this remote, rough and high-lying habitat. If those voles can survive and prosper in Kielder they'll have done tremendously well. Let's not expect them to go even further and repopulate the UK, let's give them a hand with more releases in the region, preferably within reach of one another so that populations can meet and spread the gene pool. Between them the wildlife trusts, the rivers trusts, the National Trust, Forestry England, the local councils and forward-thinking private landowners control myriad areas of land which would be favourable places for water voles, and other "lost" species to thrive in. And supportive and pro-active national governments could be pretty useful too. Less talk, more action please.

The reintroduction of water voles is only a very small, though important, piece of the whole matrix. Simply releasing voles without modification of their habitat and the control of predators would be futile. And it isn't only "invasive" species we need to be concerned with. We humans have caused a great imbalance in the natural ecosystems which exist throughout the world. Totally pristine environments are extremely rare and becoming rarer by the day. We can get excited by news of discoveries of previously-unknown flowers or frogs but as we become distracted by the beauty and wonder of such things, we might just consider what these "discoveries" tell us about the level of our ignorance of the natural world. There is still so much that we don't know and need to know if we have any chance of leaving any sort of natural world for our descendants. Having upset the balance of nature as the result of fulfilling our own needs or our own greed together with our lack of knowledge and foresight I believe as many others do, that we have another need. The need to begin to control the onslaught on nature. To rein in the destruction. To satisfy our need to repair our own morality. I am not in any way religious, a very devout atheist in fact. But I do believe that there is a social morality. An obligation to future humans and to our plant and animal relations on this planet. We are all part of the same system. We have developed and lived together on this ever-changing planet as life has arisen and grown and adapted to these changes. Either gradually or catastrophically. For the last few tens or even thousands of decades there has been a level of balance. Change has largely been driven by fluctuations in the climate or tectonic activity, even extraterrestrial events. But in the last few centuries, and particularly this last one the rate of change and the causes of it have come from a new direction. The increasing dominance over the world of *Homo sapiens*. We have the power to destroy nature and we have set about it in a systematic and selfish manner. For the majority of us this has happened without us realising what impact we are having on nature and on our own chances of surviving as a species for a bit longer. Now we need to take a more benign, and yet in some ways more controlling, hand. The preservation and regeneration of our forests, rivers, tundra and oceans depends upon us and our actions now. Next century will be too late.

So let's get back to our voles. What does this mean for them. First of all, we have to continue the good work which has begun. We have to ensure that they continue to have the conditions they need for survival. The recent changes in forestry practices have to be continued and even enhanced. As the voles thrive and spread this may cause some headaches for the forestry business. Will there be areas suitable for forestry but barred from this by the presence of the water vole. Or will they try to mitigate the impact by trapping and relocating the animals. The thought of this as standard practice worries me. I can't believe that vole populations are not traumatised and therefore damaged by this. OK as a last resort and better than simply ignoring their presence but not great.

We also need to be aware that it isn't only American mink which we need to consider. Whilst Tony Martin believes that eradicating the mink population will lead to an explosion in vole numbers as it seems to have done in East Anglia, I'm not convinced that this would be the case up in Kielder Forest. As poor old Neville would testify if he were still with us, there are lots of other threats around.

We have ample evidence that our voles are frequently part of the diet of foxes, herons, tawny owls, stoat etc. This is absolutely natural and expected. However, the numbers of these predators in the forest creates a risk, especially during the period whilst they try to get established. The absence of apex predators leaves the enemies of the vole to occupy more of the continuum than they would in the natural order. The recent example of the disappearance of the golden eagle from Haweswater in the Lake District shows how other predators thrive in their absence. Since the eagle has left the numbers of buzzards and ravens has risen. Eagles would very rarely take a water vole. Buzzards and ravens might well enjoy them.

What's the answer? I'm certainly not equipped to make any meaningful suggestion but I do feel that we need to adopt a much larger scale, landscape-wide approach wherever we can. For our voles the reintroduction of the beaver would certainly help. These fantastic water engineers would create the perfect environment. Getting more controversial would be the release of the lynx and even more controversially the wolf. Their very presence would be likely to reduce the numbers of those medium-sized vole-eating predators such as the fox and so help our releasees to have a better chance of thriving. We need to work toward a more natural balance in our remaining "wildish" areas, and to increase their area. As we begin to see this being successful maybe we can begin to relinquish some of our control and allow nature to take its course. But in my lifetime, and I suspect the next generation, we will need to manage the change sensitively.

I think it is very informative to see how we humans can retrieve controversy from something which seems straightforward. Most people probably wouldn't object to the suggestion that we could do with more natural green areas in our overcrowded island. The UK is one of the most nature-deprived countries on the globe. But when we start to implement change, things start to hot up. As Lee Schofield's excellent book "Wild Fell" illustrates beautifully, people can easily feel threatened, and our use of terminology becomes problematic. Rewilding has been bandied about a lot in recent years. To many of us this is a positive and forward-looking concept. But to your neighbouring sheep farmer it can seem to be an existential threat. It sounds like you want to ban their way of life and totally change the environment into one where they are no longer welcome. And their families may have lived and worked for generations on these very hills you want to rewild.

Kielder Wildwood has been referred to as a "reseeding" project to reflect the fact that nature is being given a helping hand to get started but that henceforward the best approach is largely hands off and let nature rebuild itself. But even so, care will be needed to ensure that populations of feral goats and roe deer don't get out of hand and that the neighbouring Sitka spruce plantations don't do too much of their own reseeding. We know they can because I have spent many days over the last few years removing Sitka spruce saplings from land which is naturally moorland or bog. Some days knee deep in water on our reserve in the Border Mires with the evocative name of "The Wou". If you can be bothered to look this up on the local OS map, you'll find the name printed in blue. As I told leader Geoff "You do realise that you're sending us into what is labelled on the map as a watercourse?" He threw me some armbands and we carried on regardless.

Whether we choose to label our activities as rewilding, reseeding, renaturing, wilding, restorative nature or whatever, I think the key to success has to be getting people on our side. Where they may feel threatened, we need to talk and persuade. Where they are uninterested and disconnected, we need to encourage and inspire. It doesn't take much to get most people excited by nature. We just need to give more people access and opportunity to get involved and to taste what could be. Although probably not on four-wheel drive or trail bike excursions over sensitive moorland. Have your fun but have it somewhere appropriate. Particularly where people's livelihoods and ways of life seem to be at risk, we need to show empathy and to model how this does not have to be the case. On a recent trip to one of the private estates in the Cairngorms we learned how the new owners and managers of the estate had to show that the loss of jobs in the deer stalking industry was more than compensated for by new jobs in conservation and recreation. Indeed, more jobs were created in stalking in order to drastically reduce the overpopulation of deer on the estate so that the native flora and fauna could flourish once again. With the reduction in red deer numbers, the numbers of ptarmigan and capercaillie increased and the juniper forest which had been thought to have disappeared raised its head above the heather once again without the threat of being browsed off. We can all be a bit browsed off with the state of nature in our country today but there are signs of hope emerging. And in order for Neville and his kind to thrive again we need to keep up the great work which so many organisations and individuals are striving to achieve.

"Animals arrived, liked the look of the place, took their quarters, settled down, spread and flourished. They didn't bother themselves about the past - they never do. They're too busy. The Wild Wood is pretty well populated now; with all the usual lot, good, bad and indifferent - I name no names. It takes all sorts to make a world."

(Wind in the Willows)

OK. But we now know water vole good, American mink bad. At least over here.
I hope the above rings true in the Kielder Forest of the not-too-distant future.

And so, as I approach the age of 75 and the prospect of middle age gets closer, I have to look back with great fondness on the best part of a decade working with the Restoring Ratty team and look forward to the next great adventure which NWT has to offer. Hope it's as good as this was. And then my mind drifts back to Briarwood and my first years with NWT. The nightmares have almost gone.

Footnote: What happened to Neville?
Of course we can never really know. If he survived that trauma in 2017, he would have been lucky to have lived for another 18 months. We could by now be encountering his 14x great grandchildren. And if he had somehow been lucky enough to have been taken to a safe place he might have lived for another couple of years. But by 2024 he would be almost 350 in *Homo sapiens* years. Unlikely you would think. So, farewell for now. I'm just going down to the garden shed with a few apple and carrot snacks…we know who likes those.

APPENDIX

1. Early Monitoring Reports.
2. Wildflower Record.
3. More Photographs.
4. Awards.
5. More Interesting Sightings.
6. List of Characters.

Appendix 1. A Sample of my Monitoring Reports.

These caused some early consternation back at base. But after a while some people began to look forward to them. See what you think.

November Mink Raft Report
21.11.16.

"Four Get Frozen in Kielder"

One of the Fabulous Four series by Edna Brighton

"Gosh", said Mel, "this water's awfully cold, Sue". "Never mind", said Sue, "we'll soon be with Queen Kelly of the Water Voles at her castle in Kielder. Don says she might have some nice tea and buns there." "Crikey", said Don, "I think you're mixed up. It's Princess Naomi of the Meadowlands who has the nice buns". Whilst all this was going on, Dave was having spiffing fun dancing in the mud. Off the jolly four went to check all of their super mink rafts, only to find that the nasty Ice Witch had been there before them. Sue was a jolly good sport opening all of the gates – Don couldn't because he had a nasty graze on his arm – until we came to those nasty metal ones. "Bugger these bloody locks!", she said. (Sue!) (More adventures of the Fabulous Four next time.)

Anyway, we got the round done in good time with no problems for once. The only issue being that all of the rafts were ice bound. The clay had frozen into various interesting patterns which would have destroyed any prints. The ground around was frozen so hard that no prints would have been made there either.

New stakes were provided for rafts 18 & 40. The clay and oasis were refreshed on rafts 3, 10 and 11.

Obviously, no sign of mink. But we did see a very handsome fox, two roe deer, a buzzard and a heron.

Sue, Mel, Dave & Don 21.11.16

13.03.2017

Vole-unteers Discover True Reason for Fall in Water Vole Numbers.

Mink Unfairly Accused of Eating Voles

For years American mink have been blamed for the demise of the water vole in Britain. (Fake news!) Our crack team of vole-unteers have discovered the truth. Using cameras carefully concealed in their bait tins, footage was obtained of the Ratty Tsar preparing her daily intake of "Vole Pies"! Having tricked her way into this powerful role, "Queen Ratty" has been able to establish her take away vole pie business (see photo of her undercover pie delivery van) throughout the region. There are rumours that she intends to expand her business into Durham! Below we can see a despairing vole-unteer inspecting his empty mink raft.

Undaunted the team continued their monitoring rounds today. No trace of mink (or water voles - not surprising!) was found.

We had a very good day, with the weather gradually improving & feeling rather like spring. Rafts 35 (Oh Me Sike), 37 (Ridge End Burn) and 19 (Irish Bridge) were finally refloated after we had negotiated the numerous hazards of logging lorries and tree-felling machinery.

Raft 11 (Humble Pond) was repaired & new clay added. Clay was also added to rafts 39 (Bull Crag), 26 (Emblehope - the raft was also repositioned on the other side of the stream to see if this will stop the clay being washed off), and 33 (Bla Wearie). Otherwise, most rafts were in good condition.

Raft 4 (Hatchery Weir) was covered in the tracks of a small mammal. Shrew or field vole? Other wildlife highlights included a red fox near Emblehope and ponds full of frogs (bird hide) and newts (Lower Scaup Pond). Several buzzards were seen & heard and the Canada geese are back on Upper Scaup Pond. Kelly was chuffed to see her first colt's-foot of the year! (Not to be confused with vole's trotters - very tasty!)

Because we were short on numbers for half of the day, rafts 25 (lily pond) and 40 (Plashetts) were not checked - although it was only a week since their relaunch. Make them a priority next time.

Next time out we need to find a new site for raft 12 (Little Whickhope) and put raft 18 (Allery Bank) back into the stream at Bower Bridge for the summer season.

John and the Ratty van.

MINK RAFT MONITORING

STRINGENT NEW TRAINING INTRODUCED FOR VOLUNTEER DRIVERS IN KIELDER FOREST

It had been a quiet & uneventful start to this mink raft monitoring round as we checked rafts 20 (Waterhead) and 14 (Black Sike). No sign of any controversial prints on raft 14 this time around. As we stood there the sound of distant chain saws drifted across to us. But these sounds seemed a bit different; higher pitched, more constant? Anyway, off we headed toward the heart of the forest and Bellingburn Head. We never made it! As we rounded a bend in the track, Sue braked hard and we screeched to a halt (quietly). The track was blocked off with hundreds of yards of tape and several vehicles. Curiously we approached an official-looking guy in his yellow hi-vis - always a good look in the forest. He turned out to be a marshal - looked a little like Wyatt Earp - on the Roger Albert Clark Rally, which was taking place all over the forest. After watching a few competitors fly past, and discussing rally manoeuvres we re-boarded our trusty Isuzu and departed. This involved Sue in some high-quality reversing to be followed by several attempts at the Scandinavian flick, the mud-slide, the spectator car tunnel and the 17-point turn. After retracing our route and with the loss of just under the hour we arrived at Bull Crag. Phew!

The rally route was encountered on several other occasions but fortunately this only resulted in the failure to check two rafts - Bellingburn Head (29) and Straight Mile Sike (50).

Sue masters the "Scandinavian flick" to improve speed & efficiency on raft monitoring round.

Apart from all of this rally excitement there isn't a lot else to report. Most exciting was the sight of water vole prints and poo on raft 43 (Archer Cleugh Pond).

As you can see in the photo below the Queen does not seem to be impressed by the poo.

Water vole prints & poo on raft 43.

Water vole prints were also seen at the wildlife hide (raft 2) and possibly on raft 8 (Upper Scaup Pond), although these were very not at all clear, but numerous.

All of the other rafts were in good condition but showing no signs of activity. NO SIGN OF AMERICAN MINK WAS SEEN.

All of our coir-based baskets were still soft and doing well. I think this is the Wendy 3 model. Further discussion took place about the possibility of replicating the use of coir in pond & stream rafts with the use of a permeable membrane. Perhaps we should try a couple in the ponds first. (The Wendy 4 is ready to launch if someone remembers to bring along a suitable liner next time out.)

We did see a few buzzards, two goosanders and several mallards but not much else. Hardly surprising considering the noise and activity generated by the rally.

Flower of the Week is suspended for the winter season, but for your pleasure we have replaced it with Fungus Fortnight. All entries are welcome. This time out it's the yellow stag's-horn (*Calocera viscosa*). Target species for the season are wood cauliflower and *Mitrula paludosa*.

26.11.19 Sue, Wendy &Mel

Appendix 2. Some of the wildflowers recorded on our trips.

Wildflowers of Kielder Forest

Autumn gentian   *Harebell aka Scottish bluebell*

Marsh violet

Once spring arrives we have been on the lookout for wildflowers and our reports often mentioned our "Flower of the Week". Unfortunately, this wasn't built into the IT-based survey system and it got a bit lost. Some of these techies lack soul. These three are amongst my favourites but there are lots of others.

Below is a list of some flowers which we recorded.

alder	forget me not - changing	red-berried elder
amphibious bistort	forget me not - field	rhododendron
angelica	foxglove	rough hawkbit
autumn gentian	germander speedwell	rowan
bedstraw - heath	goldenrod	scabious - field
bedstraw - lady's	goldilocks	St. John's wort
bedstraw - marsh	gorse	selfheal
bell heather	green figwort	silverweed
betony	groundsel	slender trefoil
birds-foot trefoil	hairy lady's-mantle	snake's-head fritillary
birds-foot trefoil - greater	harebell	skullcap
bistort	heather	sneezewort
bog asphodel	hedge woundwort	sow thistle - perennial
bottle sedge	hedge bindweed	sow thistle - prickly
bramble	heath groundsel	speedwell - heath
branched bur-reed	hemlock water-dropwort	speedwell - wood
bridewort	hemp nettle	stitchwort - greater
broad-leaved dock	herb-robert	stitchwort - lesser
broom	hogweed	tansy
bugle	horsetail	thistle - creeping
bugle - white var.	kingcup	thistle - marsh
burnet	knapweed	thistle - spear
bush vetch	knotted pearlwort	thistle - welted
buttercup - creeping	smooth lady's-mantle	three- nerved sandwort
buttercup - meadow	lesser bulrush	timothy

cat's-ear
cleavers
climbing corydalis
cloudberry
clover - red
clover - white
clover - zigzag
colt's-foot
columbine
common dog violet
common spotted orchid
cornelian cherry

corn spurrey
cotton grass – hare's-tail
cowberry

cranberry
crane's-bill - French
crane's-bill - meadow
crane's-bill - wood

creeping cinquefoil
cross-leaved heath

crosswort
cuckoo flower
curled dock
daisy
dandelion
devil's-bit scabious

lesser spearwort
lesser hop trefoil
lousewort
mallow
mare's-tail
marsh lousewort
marsh violet
marsh willowherb
marsh woundwort
meadowsweet
meadow vetchling

melancholy thistle

milkwort
mouse-ear

mouse-eared hawkweed
mullein
musk mallow

nettle

New Zealand willowherb
nipplewort
northern marsh orchid
oxeye daisy
pineapple weed
plantain - greater
plantain - ribwort
plantain - water
primrose

toadflax
tormentil
trailing tormentil
tufted vetch
tutsan
twayblade
valerian
valerian - marsh
water avens
water mint
willowherb - great

willowherb -broad-leaved

willowherb - rosebay
wood anemone

wood avens

wood sage
wood sorrel

yarrow

yellow flag iris

yellow loosestrife
yellow rattle

yellow water lily

early dog violet
early marsh orchid
enchanter's night-
shade
eyebright
fairy flax figwort

purple moor grass
ragged robin
ragwort

raspberry
red bartsia

Appendix 3. Some more photos.

American mink and a water vole.

A good comparison of size and colour. But most of our voles were darker. A very useful prop for Graham and Kelly when giving their numerous presentations.

September 2022 and our last release pen is handed over to colleagues from Cumbria.

We were delighted to see them in use in 2023.

John thinks it's all over. Resting on his trusty fisherman's stool as he contemplates the end of this part of the story.

John used to work for Yorkshire Wildlife Trust before retiring to Northumberland and joining NWT as a volunteer. He brought lots of invaluable knowledge ….and a lot of anecdotes.

Coral and her trusty cardboard tube.

Coral was our main contact with the Derek Gow Consultancy and made the long trip up from Devon year after year. She was a delight to work with and is much missed.

The interesting structure at Blakehope Nick.

Highest point on the Forest Drive and next to our raft at Bla Wearie. Designed and built by Newcastle University Architecture students and fondly known as the Bus Shelter.

John Bower and Mel put out a release pen at Upper Scaup Pond.

Appendix 4. Awards.

Congratulations to the Ratty team. 2019 saw the project win two awards. And this was after only five years! Lots more work has been done since.

First was this CIEEM (Chartered Institute of Ecology and Environmental Management) award which key team members had to travel to London to collect.

Jenny, Coral (DGC), Simon (NWT), Paul (FE), Sue, Graham, Kelly (NWT), Liz (TRT) and Tom (FE)

And not such a long trip to collect the "Love Northumberland" Award. Kelly 2nd from left and Steve on the right.

Well done to the lot of them. Especially team leaders (Ratty tsars) Kelly and Graham.

Appendix 5. The Mystery of the Archer Burn Stump.

A particular tree stump on the Archer Cleugh Burn has given us much pause for thought. Is this place of particular significance? Did the ancients worship here or have I got a fertile imagination? Whatever the reason just here we have found a number of interesting phenomena.

Astral jelly   *Anal jelly*

What's the difference between astral and anal jelly? And what have otters got to do with it? Neither of these jellies should be used in a trifle.

On the left we see **astral jelly**. A virtually colourless and transparent substance which appears occasionally and disappears very quickly. Until very recently this substance caused great puzzlement in the world of philosophers, naturalists and others. As early as the 14th century this phenomenon was thought to have been the remains of stars which had fallen to earth. Hence its alternative name of star jelly. On analysis it seemed to be inert, with no detectable DNA. So probably not related to animals. A more recent, so far unproven, theory is that this substance originates in the oviduct of frogs and toads. When predators eat such amphibians, they find that this substance is totally indigestible and it is regurgitated. If an otter for instance has been on a feeding binge when coming across large numbers of frogs making their way to the breeding grounds it will regurgitate large amounts of this jelly. As the photo shows we found a lot of it on this tree stump on a couple of occasions. And very soon it was gone.

Anal jelly on the other hand (please wash your hands after touching this) is better understood. It doesn't sound very pleasant, does it? The sample shown on the right is unusually colourless but it contains lots of DNA. It has come from the otter as a discharge. It is similar in shape and smell to otter scat (poo) but doesn't contain fur, bones, fish scales or other evidence of what it has eaten. As otters often leave their scat to mark out their territory and indicate their presence, it was once thought that this jelly was simply scat from an otter which hadn't eaten recently. More recently it has been suggested that the jelly is in fact a mucus from the intestine of the otter which protects it from sharp bones and scales and is then deposited. It can be white, as our sample, brown, orange or black. Possibly dependent upon what the animal has eaten.

So, it seems that both of the substances on our tree stump may have come from the same animal. Just from different ends. Sorry about that. I hope you weren't eating whilst reading this bit.

*But what was this? It is **hair ice.***

And near the same tree stump, but on a different occasion we came across some dead wood which looked as though it was covered in candy floss. A similar substance can be seen on the heads of several volunteers shown in the photos in this book.

I can't recall having seen it anywhere else but we have found it several times in the forest.

Hair ice needs very specific conditions.

1. Moist rotting wood from a broadleaf tree.
2. Moist air at a temperature just below freezing.
3. A fungus called *Exidiopsis effusa*.

The pores in the rotting wood are full of water. As the temperature drops the water freezes. The fungus creates a barrier between the new ice and the wood. As the ice forms it expands and the only way is up and out of the pores. This creates long thin strands of ice which can reach several centimetres in length. The hair ice - also known as beard ice - can last for several hours. But not if you pick up the branch and place it in a warm vehicle so that you can take it back to base to show the rest of the team.

And some other nice fungi:

Mitrula paludosa. *aka bog beacon.*

Found in a pond on the Bull Crag peninsula. Growing on the rotting leaves which are floating on the pond. Looks like lots of tasty orange lollipops, but very small. I was excited to see this for the first time in 2016 and the next year too. But then someone decided to clear the pond as it becoming overgrown.

Not edible.

***Sparassis crispa**. aka cauliflower fungus.*
Quite large - see the foot in the top right - growing at the base of a Lodgepole Pine. Quite tasty when fresh apparently. But needs cooking. That might be Steve Backshall's foot.

Cladonia floerkeana. aka devil's matchsticks.

Found in several places growing on the acid soils amongst the heather and sphagnum moss. Not technically a fungus but a lichen - which contains fungus, algae and bacteria.

These and lots of other fungi, along with the flowers and birds and, oh yes, trees, were a welcome distraction on our long journeys around the forest.

Appendix 6.
List of Characters. Not in any order of appearance.

The Team:
Staff:
  Graham Holyoak: Co-team leader. Formerly with Tyne Rivers Trust. Now involved with county-wide rewilding for NWT. Threw lots of tech into the project.
  Kelly Hollings: Co-team leader. There from the very start in her role with Northumbrian Water Nature Reserves. Subsequently involved with beavers and trees with the National Trust and Newcastle City Council. Very good with people and biscuits.
Katy Barke: Area co-ordinator trying to manage the above. Also into Osprey Watch and the Wildwood.
Lou Chapman: Volunteer Manager. Well, you try co-ordinating a bunch of volunteers who disappear off into Kielder Forest at the drop of a hat. How do you keep track of them?

…….and lots of others who came out to help with the water vole release weeks, especially when the press was around. Too many to mention them all but including Alice, Geoff, Dan, Duncan, Chloe etc etc.

Volunteer Leaders:
Mel Rockett: You've heard enough about me already.
Don Learmouth: ex-police driver and quarry manager. Excellent for getting us around the forest and out of tricky situations.
Sue Cornick: aka "Bins". The only one of us to have seen a golden eagle over the forest. A constant, reliable and steady member of the group. Frequent source of information about wildlife seen on her frequent trips to Scotland and beyond. Excellent poo spotter with a bridge named after her.
Dave Duffy: aka "Hides" No problems were too great for Dave. Ex-fire officer always keeping us aware of Health & Safety. Very

useful when some volunteers were out. After several years it became too much and he disappeared off in his mobile home to regain his sanity.

John Wollaston: aka "Caddis Fly". An individual sense of humour and great depth of knowledge to keep everyone amused and on their toes. Some people even came back for a second dose. Ex-field officer with Yorkshire Wildlife Trust and mushroom grower. Talk about busman's holiday.

Ellesse Janda: aka "The Influencer". Ph.D. student undertaking extensive practical experience and leading on water vole surveys for the last years of the project. Responsible for tattoos appearing on volunteers who should know better.

Steve Harris: aka "The Laminator". IT expert Steve was with us from the start but unfortunately ill health curtailed his activity soon after. But not before he had provided us with detailed maps of all our raft sites. Very fond of wild camping which made him eminently suitable for work in Kielder Forest.

Robin Bailey: aka "Birdman". Another one of the originals Robin is a great bird watcher and was a backbone of the team until relocating to the Lakes and beyond to pursue his passion. I still treasure his 2016 calendar featuring the wildlife of Madagascar. All photos taken by himself. And nor will I forget the day he was driving on the Forest Drive in the snow when we were confronted by a speeding timber lorry who had no intention of stopping!

……and again, lots of volunteers who joined us over the years. Too many to mention but special thanks to John, Simon, Ken, Wendy, Isis, Pat, Mustapha, Wendy, Jessica etc.

……. and a special mention for **Joel Ireland.** Joel spent most of 2018 with us to complete the second year of his degree course at Nottingham Trent University with a practical experience. He got it. Once he recovered from his initiation into the team Joel was a tremendous asset with his positivity, practical skills and enthusiasm.

www.ingramcontent.com/pod-product-compliance
Ingram Content Group UK Ltd.
Pitfield, Milton Keynes, MK11 3LW, UK
UKHW052348210325
5113UKWH00008B/55